Portfolios
in the Writing Classroom

Portfolios
in the Writing Classroom

An Introduction

Edited by

Kathleen Blake Yancey
University of North Carolina at Charlotte

National Council of Teachers of English
1111 Kenyon Road, Urbana, Illinois 61801

Staff Editor: Sheila Ryan

Cover Design: Carlton Bruett

Interior Design: Doug Burnett

NCTE Stock Number 36451-3050

Library of Congress Cataloging-in-Publication Data

Portfolios in the writing classroom : an introduction / edited by
 Kathleen Blake Yancey.
     p.   cm.
   Includes bibliographical references.
   ISBN 0-8141-3645-1
   1. English language—Composition and exercises—Study and teaching
—United States.   I. Yancey, Kathleen Blake, 1950–
LB1576.P66   1992
808'.042'07—dc20   91-39907
                                                                         CIP

Contents

Preface

Portfolio. For some, the word conjures up a simple manila folder that houses some sort of collection of writing. For others, the word suggests yet another educational "solution" that will disappear if we just hold our breath long enough. And for still others, the idea of the portfolio with the vagaries it seems to bring along with it—reflection and collaboration and shared authority—sounds as if it might be worth exploring.

This collection of essays argues that portfolios are indeed worth exploring and that such an exploration opens up new opportunities: new ways to learn to write; new ways to think about the teaching of writing; new ways to read and understand our students, ourselves, and our curricula; and new ways to describe and then report on what we find. The collection makes this argument by sharing the stories of teachers in various situations, from the teacher alone in his classroom, to the teacher as team member, to the teacher concerned with administration as well as learning.

Regardless of the pedagogical perspective, however, the contributors agree on several key points: that portfolios should be designed locally by teachers and students; that they require periodic review; that through this review we can learn more about writing and its teaching. This collection thus speaks most profoundly to the teacher who is still learning, who is learning with her students, and who is not afraid to make some basic changes in her classroom.

This volume came into being because there was none like it. In the spring of 1989, I returned from the Conference on College Composition and Communication in Seattle impressed particularly with what I had heard on two counts. I had heard much about teachers as agents of change, an idea I had not encountered in what seemed a very long time; and I had heard about portfolios, collections of writing used to help students and teachers write differently and read differently. Because I was working with new graduate teaching assistants and with student teachers, I wanted to share with them some of what I had learned and then ask us to expand what we knew by consulting additional resources. The resource shelf for portfolios was bare, however. This volume thus intends to address that situation and to do so in the larger context of the teacher as agent of change.

1 Introduction: Writing Portfolios—Changes and Challenges

Catharine Lucas
San Francisco State University

The chapters in this book are not about the use of portfolios for large-scale, external testing. They are not about how to test for minimum standards at middle school graduation, or for college entrance or placement, or for school accountability, or for statewide "report cards" on literacy. Instead, they are about changing what teachers and students learn from classroom writing. Although a few of the authors appearing here are known for their work in trying to make big tests better, in this volume they are speaking exclusively about the role of the portfolio within the classroom. The portfolio projects they describe are accompanied by a profound shift in attitudes toward the role of evaluation in learning. I believe this shift, far more than the practical procedures they describe for "managing" student work, accounts for the remarkable changes many of these authors observe in their classrooms.

Evaluation as Learning

As I read the pieces presented here and think of the contexts that generated them, I am persuaded that nothing since the advent of small-group collaborative learning has carried such potential to revolutionize the teaching and assessment of writing. These authors seem far less interested in the *assessment of outcomes* through comparative rankings of achievement, such as those produced by grades, test scores, and percentile rankings, than in the *enhancement of performance* through evaluative feedback and reflection. In 1967, Scriven coined the term "summative evaluation" to describe outcomes assessment that yields an external, terminal judgment, as distinct from what he calls "formative evaluation," which provides internal, continual feedback to the performer-in-action. In the chapters that follow, however, something further emerges, which we might dub "reflective evaluation," a kind of formative feedback the *learners give themselves.* The authors work from the assumption that such self-evaluation is essential to a writer's growth toward confidence and mastery, in fact is the very stuff of learning.

Summative evaluation, as a rule, can have little effect on learning, other than in some vague way, helping to ensure that students try hard, often substituting a preoccupation with high scores for a fascination with what their own minds can achieve. Yet summative assessment of outcomes constitutes the primary use of evaluation in schooling, both for its efficiency in reporting outcomes and for the indirect carrot-and-stick effect on teachers and students, as it is used in an accountability model of education. As a result, the traditional writing classroom is poorly supplied with opportunities for evaluation that actually teaches rather than merely motivates through reward and punishment.

Fortunately, the recent renaissance in composition studies has supported and extended the use of formative feedback in the writing classroom—through teacher-guided revision and peer response in small groups, activities that the best and bravest teachers have made the cornerstone of their writing programs, even where the external tests that measure their achievement contain only sudden-death impromptu essays or, worse, short-answer or multiple-choice items. The portfolio projects described in this volume belong to this larger movement toward the use of formative, internal assessment to enhance performance and growth in writing, independently of what external testers may do. They exemplify the work of teachers who have transcended "teaching to the test" and show how any teacher can use portfolios to encourage reflective evaluation among students, while any district or system can use portfolios to stimulate effective, formative, "in-process" evaluation among teachers who currently use summative or "final" grading practices as their primary mode of feedback to learners.

Why are changes like these necessary? Although summative assessment, whether it generates external test scores or classroom grades, has typically had enormous impact on the way students and teachers work and learn, it nonetheless remains, in a sense, peripheral to the learning process itself. "Winning points" may be the final goal of classroom work as it is of the sports endeavor, but the grade, like the final score of the game, never taught anyone how to win again, or why they lost. For the truly successful contenders, playing the game is always about learning the game and learning the self in the game, however often it may seem to be about scoring more wins than losses.

Caring about grades, those external stamps of approval or dis-approval that teachers rely on to motivate achievement, can go only so far to guarantee meaningful effort. Beyond the extrinsic motivation of test scores and grades must lie some intrinsic reward, some freedom to feel curiosity, if a student—or any other performer—is to muster the long-range commitment that makes deep and lasting learning possible, and with it the kind of deepening perception, steady concentration, critical thinking, and creative imagination that we hope our students will aspire to.

Promises and Pitfalls of Portfolio Practice

One can only reach out to embrace any teaching practice that, like the portfolio projects being attempted here, heightens intrinsic motivation by releasing teachers and students from the defensive stance of test takers, substituting an informed self-evaluation. Where readers are free to innovate, these practices will find eager imitators. But the larger realm of pedagogical politics and policy and the wider realities of both institutional and personal resistance to change contain a number of threats to these new ideas. While I remain confident that portfolio pedagogy will make its way by virtue of what it offers, with or without full understanding by the society at large, with or without funding in an uncertain economy, I also believe that readers might benefit from awareness of these threats as they read about and consider adopting this promising assessment and teaching tool.

To this end, by way of introduction to this book, I would like to identify briefly three challenges that must be met by the portfolio movement if its enormous potential is to be realized in the ways suggested here. Others may see additional dangers or find even these unconvincing, but my chief areas of concern are (1) the weakening of effect through careless imitation, (2) the failure of research to validate the pedagogy, and (3) the co-option by large-scale external testing programs.

Weakening of Effect

A natural threat in any grass-roots movement, when it gains real momentum, is that the initial idea and its driving principles will be so simplified and diluted during dissemination that practices bearing little or no resemblance to the original design will claim its name, and thus the movement will lose its original power to support learning. This does not mean that I am concerned about the many variations on a theme that will inevitably be required as an idea is applied in many contexts; experimentation in many settings should strengthen the pedagogy, enriching our practice and our understanding of its impact on learners, at least where we can avoid either-or thinking and polarizing debates over these variations. Rather, my concern is that portfolio pedagogy not be reduced to a set of easily described steps so that it can be taught to and required of whole faculties of teachers in one or two inservice sessions, applied top-down as a panacea, rather than growing organically out of the needs and curiosities and abilities of teachers who are ready to stretch themselves in a new way. This danger is not necessarily fatal, but it can attenuate the special benefits of the pedagogy.

I think of the recent history of collaborative learning or small-group pedagogy as demonstrating both the weakening effects of band-wagoning and the resilience of a really good idea. When I began teaching twenty-five years ago, the idea of using small groups as a pedagogical tool was just filtering into the profession, where only a few of the most progressive practitioners were discovering how independent learning groups or student collaboration could revolutionize their teaching. In the years since, I have watched collaborative learning become accepted as basic pedagogy in the most conservative schools of education. But in observing other teachers, both novice and experienced, I continue to be amazed at how many things "small-group instruction" can mean, at how many ways—helpful and unhelpful—it can be implemented, and at how little we really know about when, why, or how it works best and for whom. I am most of all struck by how little the "new pedagogy" changes things unless teachers are willing to change more than how they arrange the desks and chairs.

It is probably not possible to forestall the bandwagon effect with its resultant misuse or superficial application of portfolio pedagogy, if only because people everywhere follow the fashion. Teachers will undoubtedly come under pressure to try portfolios if administrators get the notion that they might work. And for every teacher who resists change, there is another who loves the fads, fresh ideas to inject into Monday mornings. But how might the conscientious teacher avoid following the fad and reach instead for the more subtle and lasting rewards of portfolio pedagogy as it is described in this volume? I am reminded of a colleague's conversation with a student who said, "I'll do anything for an *A*." "Anything?" she replied. "Yes, anything. Just name it!" he exclaimed. "Would you consider studying?"

Learning to "do it right," to integrate this process into one's classroom, live with it through its failures and misfires, hone it, adapt it, transform it, requires really studying, not just being willing to offer it some time. The pieces in this book document the rewards of studying, showing how teachers discover the principles that make a portfolio more than a file folder of student stuff—what Newkirk (Chapter 4) calls "another kind of wastebasket." Only time will tell whether the enthusiasm expressed here is justified by something inherent in the use of portfolios: to what extent will the presence of portfolios in the classroom act on all teachers and students so that teachers who embrace this cumbersome act of "collecting student work" will find themselves forced to make of it something more?

Murphy and Smith (Chapter 6) suggest that a major advantage of portfolios is that they integrate good assessment and good teaching practice, performing this neat trick almost inevitably. I suspect that, as with small-group pedagogy, some teachers will use portfolios to integrate pedagogy and assessment more effectively than other teachers. The hope is that all who try portfolios in the classroom and study them will learn from the experiment and be changed by it. To this end, it will be essential that, just as with small-group pedagogy, teachers use existing networks to exchange ideas and critique their own practice. I hope there will be more books like this one, and conference presentations, and ethnographic research of the kind, for instance, that is slowly building understanding of what can go wrong as well as right with peer editing groups (see, for example, Freedman 1987).

The danger of losing the power of the portfolio through careless dissemination strengthens the temptation to develop a "foolproof" portfolio system to offer all teachers. But this constitutes another threat to a working portfolio classroom. The kind of portfolio project celebrated in these pages is not directly transportable across contexts, but rather depends for its life on grass-roots creativity and commitment, on evolving to serve within a specific and unique context. In her closing chapter, editor Yancey neatly extracts key principles that run through the contributions, but these all reflect ways of protecting diversity, with coherence developing within, not across, situations. Whether the portfolio concept is introduced from inside, as in the case of Gold (Chapter 3), or from outside—by a university professor in the case of D'Aoust (Chapter 5), or by researchers in the case of Murphy and Smith (Chapter 6) and Camp (Chapter 7), or by school administrators or writing program directors in the case of Newkirk (Chapter 4), Kneeshaw (Chapter 8), and Weiser (Chapter 9)—the decisions are made by teachers who are given an opportunity to "study" portfolios, experimenting to find the right choices for their own classrooms and programs.

Readers of this book will begin to identify decisions they must make to fit their own contexts: Shall I distinguish between the "display portfolio" and the "working portfolio," use all the student's work or only some? Shall our portfolio project reflect only the curriculum in each class, or in English classes across several years, or in classes across the disciplines? If we install portfolios in our whole program, do we design assignments collectively? Do we work individually or in teams when we evaluate the finished products? What kinds of information shall I attempt to extract and summarize for my own, my colleagues', or institutional purposes? How will I determine the effects that my portfolio pedagogy has on my students?

It is true that few of the teachers described here could have predicted what they would learn when they let portfolios in the door. Yet precisely because nowhere did anyone say, "Here's exactly what you must do; now do it," the learning is still going on. Can this spirit of exploration remain central to the use of portfolios as they become more commonplace? What I read here suggests that there's hope.

Failure of Research to Validate the Pedagogy

Because portfolios enter the classroom as assessment tools, and because they require no special funding, perhaps portfolio innovators will not be subjected to demands for proof of efficacy by those bent on determining whether the portfolio idea is worthy of dissemination as a classroom practice. But claims like those made in this book, testimonials of those who find portfolios transformative as a pedagogical innovation, will no doubt attract the attention of teacher educators and administrators who want research to help them answer the funding questions: Should inservice time be provided for this new fad? Should it become part of teacher training programs? Which kind of portfolio is "best" to support?

If such research is demanded by administrators before they will encourage teachers to try portfolio pedagogy, we can expect little support for the new idea. The failure of such research to identify and confirm the "worthiness" of a complex new pedagogy generally results from two factors. First, survey research is weakened by hasty and careless dissemination, so that self-reported users of "portfolios" may mean many different things by the term, with other variables affecting learning far more consistently, canceling out any apparent effects of portfolio use. Second, quasi-experimental research methodology that attempts to compare such complex behaviors as writing outcomes is notoriously reductionist, generally limited to only short-range effects and subject to many threats to validity (see Campbell and Stanley 1963; Campbell 1978).

The danger here is that those who cling to the illusion that only what can be measured or counted is worth doing will find the effects of portfolios in the classroom not only resistant to measurement but initially resistant even to definition. In time, perhaps, as the literature on the uses of portfolios expands, distinctions can be made, hypotheses generated, and theories tested. But these are early days still, and the kind of research needed—like the portfolios themselves—is driven less by ambition to affect outcomes than by curiosity to observe what those outcomes might be. Ethnographic research that "looks into" the portfolios rather than attempts to prove them worthwhile will be an essential part of the portfolio movement. The definitive, applied research that evaluates the portfolio as pedagogy will have to wait for portfolios to sort themselves out.

Co-option by Large-Scale External Testing Programs

Although classroom portfolios may not wait for research to reveal their efficacy as pedagogy, they are themselves important new tools for evaluation research and have begun to earn a place in the movement to reform large-scale writing assessment, a development many see as positive. I would like to look rather closely, however, at the potential incompatibilities between large-scale portfolio testing and the use of portfolios in the classroom.

The old debate over the relative virtues of "direct" versus "indirect" measures of writing has in recent years shifted ground, from a primary concern with the scientific properties of the measures to a primary concern with the effects of assessment on instruction. Traditionally, external testing for accountability places its faith in the indirect effects of assessment on instruction, relying on the carrot-and-stick metaphor. In this model, policymakers use tests to determine, as scientifically as possible, how well schools—their teachers and their students—are doing. Then they attempt to implement remedies: rewards, restrictions, staff development, curriculum reform, and the like, accompanied by further testing. The test is meant to provide an objective indicator of achievement: by students, by teachers, by schools or districts. Accountability testing offers evidence to taxpayers that money is well spent, and information to policymakers about what is working best or least. And when rewards are attached to successful test outcomes, everyone naturally tries to get better scores, presumably by doing a better job, by working harder. What exactly they are working at is, ideally, established independently of the test, which is intended merely to register their success.

The difficulty with this scenario has by now been pointed out by commentators (for example, Brown 1986; Chachkin 1989; Keech 1983; Lucas 1988a, 1988b). The testing program, rather than measuring outcomes, inevitably begins to shape them, and not always in positive ways. Under pressure to perform well on the measure, many teachers "teach to the test," accepting its content as a guide to curriculum, its item formats as models for classroom activities.

Currently, several assessment reform movements, acknowledging these realities of pedagogical politics, are working to create "tests worth teaching to." I have traced elsewhere (1988a) the debates that have challenged large-scale testers to take fuller responsibility for their impact on curriculum, both indirect and direct. For such assessments, the writing portfolio holds out promise as a kind of ultimate assessment tool, a test device that could inspire a full writing curriculum in classes where too little is now attempted, while for the first time adequately sampling and evaluating the achievements of teachers and students who participate in rich writing programs. But, like other attempts to reform large-scale direct assessment, the portfolio as a test represents a double-edged sword: it can liberate or oppress curricula. To the extent that the tasks included in the portfolio are narrowly set and standardized, to reduce the "messiness" of the data and make performance more comparable from student to student, the portfolio will, like other external tests before it, dictate rather than reflect curriculum. And to the extent that the pieces collected are written "for the test" rather than for the learners and their audiences, the opportunities for students to engage in purposeful task definition, reflection, and self-evaluation will be truncated.

Many of those committed to large-scale testing for accountability or for certification are already exploring how to make the portfolio concept more manageable, less messy, more cost-effective. Their efforts are no doubt valuable and may in time result in more valid measures of the complex abilities required to write well in various situations. But the worth of such portfolios, like other kinds of essay tests before them, is likely to be measured in terms of whether this cumbersome and expensive method of evaluating writing skill adds significantly to the predictive validity of a short-answer, machine-scored test. The predominant question will be, "How little writing can we collect without compromising the measure?'' (Breland et al. 1987). These pioneers of portfolio assessment are wrestling with how to reduce differences among individual portfolios and how to find common assignments and clearly defined criteria that teachers might ''teach to'' in preparation for evaluation by outsiders. They are worried about how to train readers to rate portfolios consistently. They are worried about how to restrict and control the conditions under which writing is produced, to guard against plagiarism, or unfair advantaging of some students over others. Although some portfolio assessment research is laudable for preserving the ''messiness'' of the data, a few test publishers are offering ''portfolio packages'' intended to make assessment neat and simple, its scores as reliable as other published tests of literacy. What this means in fact is that they will be just as likely as other standardized tests to limit learning by restricting curriculum to what is most easily and economically measured.

Portfolios for Ecological Evaluation

I have elsewhere (1988b) argued for the need to recontextualize literacy assessment, turning our energies from perfecting the external test toward improving evaluation in the classroom. Thinking of the classroom as an ecosystem of sorts, I have called for ''ecological evaluation'' to replace accountability testing. What I am naming ''ecological evaluation'' is much like what Wiggins is calling ''authentic assessment'' (1989) and what Guba and Lincoln have identified as ''fourth generation evaluation'' (1989). All of us are recommending classroom-based assessment dedicated to directly enhancing learning, with the assessment of outcomes for purposes of accountability occurring only as a by-product.

The portfolios discussed in these chapters belong to the emerging practices of ecological evaluation. They are based on a model that allows direct rather than indirect effects of assessment on learning: teachers and students are daily involved in formative evaluation of the writer's work, developing goals and criteria for success, informing a growing curiosity about what makes writing work in different communicative contexts. The special, arhetorical context of the *test* is replaced by a variety of contexts, opportunities to write that shape pieces of writing and writers as they will continue to be shaped throughout life.

The experience of being tested, in the sense of being stretched and challenged, is not replaced in the portfolio classroom or in life, even if tests and summative grades on essays are replaced by ongoing formative evaluation. Each time one attempts something new or difficult, one is testing oneself. And the experience of being judged, of performing for evaluators, is also not replaced. The portfolio classroom does not deny the students a summative evaluation of their work; it simply introduces formative evaluation and moves it to a new level of importance where the students' own evaluative acuity is allowed to develop.

Fortunately, large-scale portfolio use for external testing will be a long time coming, if at all. In times of restricted budgets for schools, the costs are prohibitive. Even should a windfall suddenly allow massive experimentation with the new "measurement," however, that experimentation will depend heavily on—and will contribute mightily to—teacher knowledge, as test makers design and score the multiple essays. In all the essay testing of the last two decades, widespread team scoring has inevitably raised the consciousness of teachers called upon to read for the test. And this army of increasingly aware writing teachers will, in the last analysis, be the only and best safeguard against oversimplification and overstandardization of tasks. But can the decontextualized portfolio of the external test ever serve the richer purposes of the contextualized classroom portfolio? I think not.

We can only hope that economic limitations, so often the enemy of our dreams, may in this instance serve to support the move toward school-based assessment programs, where teachers first learn to "report in"—to use systematic and collaborative evaluation efforts for their own portfolio research, to benefit themselves by looking at the data first—before they have to "report out" results to administrators and the public. With assessment recontextualized through the writing portfolio, we make room for more of the unexpected benefits of portfolio assessment-as-pedagogy, as students reclaim their work, seeing their true goals as authors to be more than pleasing a teacher or a tester.

The portfolio, like small groups, can belong to anyone's pedagogy, anyone's community of teachers and learners and researchers and evaluators. And anyone who uses it can become a teacher of other users. This book helps to begin that mutual teaching. It offers an introduction to a pedagogy, not merely to an assessment tool. It brings the reader the documented experience, with reflective commentary, that constitutes a good portfolio: there are stories, and there are interpretations of those stories. It is the kind of volume that teachers once needed to read about small groups (and perhaps still need). Those of us who are converts, or merely intrigued, willing to try, need to hear many versions of what the new pedagogy is, how it is applied by others in a range of classroom settings for a range of purposes. These authors share a vision of the portfolio as belonging to teacher and learner, not to administrator or policymaker; their goal is to cease finally to conduct learning in the service of evaluation and to commence instead to conduct evaluation in the service of learning.

References

Breland, H. M., R. Camp, R. Jones, M. Morris, and D. Rock. 1987. *Assessing Writing Skill.* Research Monograph No. 12. New York: College Entrance Examination Board.

Brown, R. 1986. "A Personal Statement on Writing Assessment and Education Policy." In *Writing Assessment: Issues and Strategies,* edited by K. Greenberg, H. Wiener, and R. Donovan. New York: Longman.

Campbell, D. 1978. "Qualitative Knowing in Action Research." In *The Social Contexts of Method,* edited by M. Brenner, P. Marsh, and M. Brenner. London: Croom Helm.

Campbell, D., and J. Stanley. 1963. "Experimental and Quasi-Experimental Designs for Research on Teaching." In *Handbook of Research on Teaching,* edited by N. L. Gage. Chicago: Rand McNally.

Chachkin, N. J. 1989. "Testing in Elementary and Secondary Schools: Can Misuse Be Avoided?" In *Test Policy and the Politics of Opportunity Allocation: The Workplace and the Law,* edited by B. Gifford. Boston: Kluwer Academic Publishers.

Freedman, S. W. 1987. "Peer Response Groups in Two Ninth-Grade Classrooms." Center for the Study of Writing, Technical Report No. 12. Berkeley: University of California Graduate School of Education.

Guba, E., and Y. Lincoln. 1989. *Fourth Generation Evaluation.* Newbury Park, Calif.: Sage Publications.

Keech, C. [C. Lucas]. 1983. "Measuring Improvement in Writing: Some Cautions." *Notes from the National Testing Network in Writing,* January, p. 3.

Lucas, C. 1988a. "Toward Ecological Evaluation." *The Quarterly* 10(1):1–17.

———. 1988b. "Toward Ecological Evaluation: Recontextualizing Literacy Assessment." *The Quarterly* 10(2):4–17.

Scriven, M. 1967. "The Methodology of Evaluation." In *Curriculum Evaluation,* edited by R. E. Stake. American Educational Research Association Monograph Series on Evaluation, No. 1. Chicago: Rand McNally.

Wiggins, G. 1989. "A True Test: Toward More Authentic and Equitable Assessment." *Phi Delta Kappan* 70(9):703–4.

2 Teachers' Stories: Notes toward a Portfolio Pedagogy

Kathleen Blake Yancey
University of North Carolina at Charlotte

This collection of essays on portfolio assessment began for several reasons. In part, it began as an effort to tease out and then articulate all those ways or reasons that explain how and why portfolios have invigorated our classrooms. And in part it began so that we could share with others what we have learned so far, in the hope that they too can learn with us as we tell our stories. But, like other teachers and writers before them, the authors who contributed to this collection did so for yet another, rather simple reason—not so much to write essays extolling the virtues of portfolios, but rather to tell a story, our own story. As English teachers, we like to tell stories, stories about our successes and our failures, stories about what we have learned already and about what we hope to learn tomorrow, and in this case particularly, stories about how we learned with our students, about how they became better, more insightful writers and we became better teachers. We value our stories, just as we value the students and teachers they remember. In their details, in the truths they embody, our stories seem to validate our experiences, to somehow make them real and to make them signify.

The stories told in this collection have a common subject, of course—portfolios—but the variations on that subject are rich and colorful. As described here, portfolios are not uniform or standardized, but diverse. They are defined variously as cultural artifacts, as collection devices, as instruments of process, as assessment tools, as means of education reform, as resources for teachers, as pictures of and guides for curriculum. In talking about portfolios, the authors also talk about nearly everything having to do with school—with new ways of teaching, new ways of seeing; with teachers changing their classes and their teaching; with students contributing to their own writing assessment. Likewise, teachers tell about different models for portfolio projects, about ways to start simple and build to something new, about new kinds of assignments and responses to writings, about understanding the kinds of reflection and behaviors that students will need to learn in order to practice portfolio assessment, about new kinds of collaboration not only among students, but also between students and teachers. They tell about authority and responsibility, making clear the threads binding them and us together.

Variations like these are made possible in part because of the diverse backgrounds of the contributors themselves. All have been or currently are teachers, most at middle and secondary schools; many have administrative experience; two are evaluation researchers; several are connected with the National Writing Project; and several are involved in teacher education. The result is that the chapters that follow include competing as well as complementary perspectives.

Although each chapter can be read independently, the arrangement of the chapters suggests the emergence of a portfolio pedagogy, taking place in classrooms where teachers and students work together on processes and products, where learning through and with writing may be the primary product. Collectively, the chapters reflect a movement from the self-initiated use of portfolios, as narrated in Sue Ellen Gold's chapter, and from the individual struggling to make sense out of a general "assignment" to introduce portfolios, as described by James Newkirk, toward the use of portfolios taken up by teachers working together in community. Catherine D'Aoust's teachers are still working individually, but support each other in a university seminar on "Teachers as Researchers." Sandra Murphy and Mary Ann Smith describe a middle school faculty cooperating with outside researchers to learn how to derive insights from a shared portfolio project—insights about students and about how portfolio projects work.

Roberta Camp's portfolio project grew out of cooperation between theorists, educational testers, administrators, and teachers of the performing arts, for whom portfolios took on a special function as instruments for student growth, allowing assessment of the learning processes as well as the products. In a sense, this piece is pivotal because it reflects the most intimate effects of a portfolio class, while representing a coherent, programmatic use of portfolios to shape pedagogy and assess learning.

David Kneeshaw discusses portfolios from an even larger perspective in his description of the Ontario "Writing Folder" project, intended to allow evaluation and record-keeping as a student moves across grade levels, but designed as well to encourage much of the same sense of discovery by teachers and students that characterizes the individual accounts. Building continuity across grades and schools, these folders, with their general assignment guidelines and instructive observations about writing processes, do not have the effect of standardizing curriculum, but rather allow teachers to shape students' writing tasks each year by encouraging growth in new areas.

Irwin Weiser tells the last story, of a considered decision to introduce portfolios into the basic writing program at Purdue University, primarily as a way to defer summative grading. Like the other authors, he reports unexpected rewards as teachers accommodate the deferred grades by learning to make more precise and helpful responses on essays. These stories are supported as well by Sheila Ewing's annotated bibliography (see Appendix), which lists resources that teachers and administrators will find useful.

This volume concludes, in Chapter 10, with some assertions about the characteristics of portfolios as artifacts within the American culture. Taken together, characteristics such as "demonstration of talent" and "range of content" provide a model that teachers may draw on and modify and redefine when they design their own projects for the classroom. The projects described here changed over time as well, through student reaction and suggestion, teacher collaboration, and the practice afforded in trial and error. Still, when we reflect on these individual projects, various as they are, we see traits that they share, a set of characteristics common to them all, qualities such as shared authority, qualitative and thoughtful response, and a commitment to development of processes over time. Collectively, then, a set of characteristics seems to be emerging, defining features of what we might call a portfolio pedagogy. In this chapter, by way of introduction and on the basis of the readings that follow, I will tentatively describe this pedagogy. Then, in the final chapter, I will broaden the context, examining portfolios in the larger culture and offering some rudimentary analysis of how and why they work in the writing class, listing key characteristics that can be extracted from the intervening chapters.

A Portfolio Classroom

A portfolio classroom is one informed by models. Initially, teachers tend to work from general models found within the culture at large, those in fine arts, for instance. In designing their classroom portfolio projects, then, teachers have taken the general models and modified them. Even after they had developed classroom portfolio models, however, teachers here realized that the new models were in process, in response to student input, to changing circumstances, to new insights.

Now, various models of classroom portfolios exist, from the model of portfolios driven by reflection, described by Camp, to the peer-response-oriented model developed by Gold. These models exhibit different relationships to the overall curriculum. Sometimes they are an integral part, as in the case of Basic Writers at Purdue and Newkirk's eighth graders; other times the portfolios play an important but not a dominating role in the class, as in some of the situations described by Murphy and Smith. Sometimes, as in the case of the ESL teacher described by D'Aoust, portfolios are not used for assessment in any institutional sense at all. And still other times, the portfolio is not only a classroom entity, but also a systemwide vehicle for teaching and curricular improvement, as is the case in Ontario. In brief, the models for portfolio assessment and practice all respond to the needs of a particular context, and they themselves are in process.

Because they are created and used in context, these classroom portfolio projects are highly individualized, intended to serve the learning needs of the students in a particular classroom who are working with a particular teacher. The projects presented here tend to be individualized in yet another way. Because they are a collection of writings, portfolios have a pattern and coherence that express or profile each individual writer, even when the contents are specified and the assignments standardized. In other words, by their very nature portfolios make possible the developmental charting of individuals, as well as a rich portrait of the writer composing for several occasions—either over a single school term (Gold, for example) or over the course of a child's schooling (Kneeshaw, for example).

A portfolio pedagogy is sensitive to process, and we see this in several ways. First, without neglecting the product that a writer creates, a portfolio pedagogy, as Camp illustrates, seeks to include and to validate processes used to create it. Accordingly, within a portfolio classroom it is commonplace to ask students to include evidence of various processes that contribute to a single work: note-taking, brain-storming, looping, drafting, redrafting in response to review, for instance. This evidence is valued for what it says about ways that the writer approaches the task and ways that the writer is developing cognitively, as well as for the part it plays in the composing of any one specific piece.

Second, of special importance in a portfolio pedagogy are two processes, *reflection* and *inquiry*. As D'Aoust suggests, one distinction between a storage folder and a portfolio is *reflection,* the review and consideration and narration and analysis and exploration of what learning is occurring in writing. As noted earlier, sometimes that reflection is the driving force in the portfolio program, as in Arts PROPEL portfolios; in others it plays a less central role. What seems important is that, within a portfolio pedagogy, reflection apparently always plays a role of some sort and is directed toward a body of work over time—made possible in part by the portfolio.

What also seems important in the reflection is the interplay between intuition and cognition. As Camp asserts, it is through reflection that students have the opportunity to play out intuitions, to consider their impact, to assess their contribution to any piece, to one kind of writing especially, and to composing generally. It may be, then, that one of the chief benefits of reflection is its role in bringing intuition both into focus and into the composing classroom.

Another process that is prized in portfolio pedagogy is *inquiry,* an exploring into writing and thinking that students and teachers undertake together. A commitment to inquiry means that no one party to the exploration knows the answers definitively or ideally, that all parties work together to negotiate meaning, and that making meaning is the enterprise shared by all. Process in itself, then, and the processes of reflection and inquiry in particular are crucial components in a portfolio classroom.

Both inquiry and reflection contribute to learning, and the learning in a portfolio pedagogy requires that everyone participate. Students in this classroom are required to be active learners, they must make choices that will affect and direct their learning, and they will learn more or less in part according to the choices they make. They are participants in the classroom, not just to help the teacher help them—though that too is important—but also to help themselves. Put differently, they are responsible for their own learning. And teachers in a portfolio pedagogy are responsible for helping students learn how to identify goals as well as to achieve them. Furthermore, in this pedagogy, teachers are also learners. They learn with their students how we all become (better) writers, how we help each other in that quest, and how we can create an environment that supports that learning.

Learning in a portfolio pedagogy is also understood to be time-intensive. It does not just happen in a day, and it does not even necessarily happen when we anticipate and prepare for it. So the gift of time, spent wisely, is central to the pedagogy. Time permits the sustained activity characteristic of portfolios, the time to compare composings, to review past goals, to match objectives with performance. Time permits the sustained dialogue within a peer group, the collaboration between student-writer and teacher-reader over the course of a term or a year, the multiple readings that any portfolio might have. Simply put, the gift of time allows students to learn to become writers, rather than to learn to write papers.

In a portfolio pedagogy, the audiences are many—the writer himself or herself, the writer's peers, the teacher. Sometimes, as in the case of Gold's model of portfolios, the teacher does not even join the audience until very late in the process. So the concept of audience takes on a new and a real meaning, both for the writer of discourse and for its readers. In some ways, this new audience is a threatening discovery because, if taken seriously, it changes the relationship among teachers and learners. At least in the old writing classroom, when the teacher is the examiner (Britton et al. 1975), there is a right answer, if only the writer can guess it. But as Murphy and Smith point out, in a portfolio pedagogy Britton's teacher-as-examiner no longer applies. Teachers are one among other members of the audience. Admittedly, they can be the preferred members of the audience—they do give out the grades, after all. But frequently, as Newkirk argues, even grading is a shared enterprise, another form of making meaning.

A portfolio pedagogy can also be somewhat threatening in the kinds of disclosure that it relies upon. Simply put, this pedagogy claims that, when teachers and students identify efforts as *both* successes and failures, writers improve. Most of us do not mind pointing to our successes, but we are not always so comfortable in acknowledging our failures, failures that perhaps no one else would even have spotted had we not identified them ourselves. This pedagogy thus assumes that writers will experience both success and failure, that both are part of being a writer, and that discussion of both is crucial for development.

As almost all the authors here have noted, these assumptions, and the teacher-student relationships they invoke, are not what students are used to, are not what teachers are used to, and are likely to make students and teachers feel fairly vulnerable, at least at first. Should students accept us at our word and admit that they did not start working until ten o'clock the night before (and weaken forever their chances of apple polishing)? Will we really not take advantage of their pointing out to us their less successful efforts? Questions like these are natural within a portfolio classroom. So too is the need for teachers and students to practice the art of being honest but not hurtful, as Camp expressed it, in setting goals, in working together, in assessing progress. Teachers too may hear a comment or two that could bruise, and like Gold, when they ask for honesty, they respect it. For it is through honesty and through discussion that meaning is shaped.

And last but certainly not least, a portfolio pedagogy defines "authentic assessment" (Wiggins 1989) in new ways. Most obvious, perhaps, is the shift from assessment of single standardized pieces to assessment of multiple, often unlike pieces of writing. These data are, in a word, messy, and they do not make evaluation any easier. According to portfolio proponents, however, they do make it valid, and they do connect assessment to learning. As writers respond to different tasks under different conditions and for different occasions, their writings (like writings we find in the "real" world) no longer look alike. There is not necessarily any one scoring guide or rubric to guide the reader seeking to compare the differing pieces of a single author, the portfolios of a single class, or the sets of portfolios belonging to a school system. But comparing students one to the next has not been a primary objective of the authors here. Rather, they have been interested in learning with the students how they develop and perform as writers.

Less obvious, but more compelling perhaps, are other changes in the ways that assessment is defined within a portfolio pedagogy. Assessment is no longer seen as a process where one party submits his or her work to another with no influence on how the work is performed or interpreted. Rather, in a portfolio pedagogy, assessment is seen as a process in which all the parties are *bona fide* participants, and in which the person whose performance is being assessed is more than an object of someone else's perusal. Students are to help define the rhetorical tasks, whether those tasks be single writing tasks or a yearlong developmental task. These tasks, then, provide part of the context in which the student's work is to be assessed. In addition, the student is often invited to narrate or to gloss the contents of the portfolio, to show how these pieces exhibit development or insight or even mistakes the writer would no longer make. In other words, this commentary provides another context in which to read the work, and its intent is to help the reader interpret the writing and the progress it represents in a way compatible with the writer's aims. To put it in Kneeshaw's terms, assessment within a portfolio pedagogy, as in other forms of assessment, operates on a kind of bias, and in this case it is "biased for best."

A portfolio pedagogy supports an open classroom and relies upon a genuinely academic environment, a place where everyone has a part to play. It is a place where all writers can succeed, and where success is directed in part by the student. It is a place where process is emphasized, where learning is always a goal for teacher and student alike. And as the following chapters demonstrate, it is a place still in the process of being shaped.

References

Britton, J. N., T. Burgess, N. Martin, A. McLeod, and H. Rosen. 1975. *The Development of Writing Abilities (11–18)*. London: Macmillan Education Ltd.

Wiggins, G. 1989. "A True Test: Toward More Authentic and Equitable Assessment." *Phi Delta Kappan* 70(9):703–4.

3 Increasing Student Autonomy through Portfolios

Sue Ellen Gold
Irvine High School
Irvine, California

With a deep sigh I turned the final page, sat back, and stared at the stack of folders sitting in front of me. The papers I had just finished reading varied widely, but were creative, thought provoking, entertaining, polished. They were, above all, clearly the work of "real" writers: ninth graders, thirty-seven fourteen- and fifteen-year-olds who had been coerced into humoring me and participating in a new project. And now, at midnight, June 23, after long months of planning, I had the hoped-for answer—portfolios work.

Several years ago I could not have said that. When Catherine D'Aoust, my instructor for the "Teacher as Researcher" class at the University of California, Irvine, first suggested designing a portfolio project, I created a cross-curricular experiment involving both the English and social science departments. Instead of being a simple study, mine had a complex, multiteacher framework. In brief, I had asked the students to bring their social science writing into my English classroom and to use their portfolios—the writings in them—as a tool to improve their writing in other content areas. Unfortunately, blending the needs of two departments and several teachers was even more difficult than I had imagined. Instead of focusing on portfolios and composing, the students and I ended up struggling to balance demands created by the conflicts of different teacher personalities and multiple curricula. I realized, however, that even though the project had floundered, the idea of portfolios had merit.

Moreover, I was not completely frustrated with my initial use of portfolios. Simply by introducing portfolios into the classroom, I had encouraged students to write more. Equally important to me, although students had written more, I had not graded more. With these insights, then, and the beginning of a new school year, I was ready to try again.

To do that, I needed to redefine not only what I hoped to achieve by using portfolios, but exactly what my students' portfolios would be. Unfortunately, I did not envision portfolios reducing my paper load. Instead, my goal was to allow the students increased autonomy and to encourage them to experiment, to risk, and to *enjoy* writing. My ninth graders' portfolios would not be filled with mandatory analytical papers, but with the students' own writings over which they had real ownership. Without the fear of imminent teacher assessment and critique, students would perhaps be able to experiment with style and voice and would learn to assess their own progress.

The Project Design

After hours of debate in the research class, I finally settled on the following guidelines for my classroom:

1. A portfolio is a folder where students store pieces of writing at various stages of completion.
2. Unlike a professional portfolio, a student portfolio should contain lots of writing, not just the finished pieces.
3. From the portfolio, students may eventually choose samples of their work to demonstrate their breadth and accomplishments as writers.

With these thoughts in mind, I began to redesign a project to fit portfolios into my class and to assess their effect. To avoid the previous year's problems, this project was to be the essence of simplicity. The overall design required the students to bring in twenty pieces of writing—one each Monday—and deposit them in their portfolios; subject, style, and form were open to their individual decisions. Every second week, the students were to choose one piece to share with peer writing groups. At the end of the semester, the students were to select three pieces as representative of their work, explain their selection process, and turn everything in as a packet for credit and evaluation.

I planned to assess the effectiveness of students' portfolios according to three criteria:

1. Their metacognitive responses to questions about portfolio use
2. Their ability to make thoughtful choices for assessment
3. Their effectiveness as writers

And so I was ready to begin once more. The project seemed easy, neat, and not too disruptive of the required ninth-grade curriculum. Because my department had made a commitment to cover the same works of literature and to assign the same number and types of essays to each student, I did not feel free to substitute the portfolio writing for any preexisting assignment. Rather, the portfolio writing had to be completed as additional work. I also anticipated that increasing the amount of writing would not endear me to the students. So the most important step still remained: to convince the students that the effort required to keep a portfolio would be worth it.

Student Response to the Portfolios

To introduce the portfolios, I explained that, in addition to completing the reading and essays assigned in the standard syllabus, students would be composing a portfolio of outside writing. Each week they were to find something that sparked their imagination, sympathy, or indignation and then write about it. Many of these pieces would be shared with peer groups, but none would be "scored" or evaluated during the semester. Instead, the students would continue to file their pieces until June, when they would choose several for grading. After finishing the overview, I asked the students to write their first reactions to the idea of keeping portfolios.

They looked at me measuringly, skeptically. Forty-five minutes into class, and I was pushing them to take a risk. "Don't worry," I added. "None of the comments will be graded, nor will I use them to make judgments about you as students. Please be honest." Because I was desperately interested in their reactions, I read many of their responses that afternoon.

The first reply was short and to the point: "I hate the idea of doing a portfolio," Ryan wrote. Nick, a recent transfer from another school, went further: "I don't want to do all these writings because (1) I never was a good writer, (2) I have always felt writing is a waste of time, (3) I'm afraid I'll be behind the other students." Melissa, meanwhile, was concerned that a portfolio "was just something else to worry about," and even Angie, the type of *A* student who wants extra credit so that she can earn an *A*+, wrote, "Why am I doing this? It will be *sooo* boring."

I had asked for, and received, honesty. So at least I knew what I was up against. It was no surprise when the first week's papers reflected the students' skepticism. After all, they had enjoyed nine years of training that equated "important" with "graded." If these pieces were not to be evaluated, then the underlying message was that composing this portfolio was busywork. Many of the students brought in half-hearted, shoddy pieces that seemed to mock the whole usefulness of portfolios. One student even wanted to get portfolio credit for an in-class note she had just written to another student complaining about having to draft a creative piece of writing!

In general, though, students' attempts to meet the portfolio requirement minimally were easy to subvert. I simply circled the classroom, glancing at papers and marking them "inadequate" when the writing seemed thrown together, poorly presented, or carelessly constructed; then I insisted that these be re-done. So, many took their "inadequate" writing home and wrote again. In addition, I periodically rechecked the work so that the students would understand that, although not yet an evaluator, I was still interested. Other than these requirements, I left the students free to create.

Portfolios and Writing Groups

The next step was getting the students and the portfolios ready for writing groups. Although some professional writers can sustain writing in a vacuum, these student writers badly needed an audience—an audience that was *not* me. Trying to balance writing strengths, gender, and ethnicity, I assigned the students to writing groups. Every second week they met with their group for one class period. During the first couple of meetings, when I insisted that the students give only positive feedback, their comments were tenuous. One student would read his or her piece, and then each group member would "comment," often merely repeating "I liked it," or "It was good." My first goal was to get them comfortable with each other, yet frustrated enough to demand critique. As I had hoped, they soon tired of unfailing gentleness, and when I asked them to write me individual notes telling me how their group was working, I received a stack of annoyed letters. "When are they going to stop telling me how *good* my writing is and start giving me something I can use?" complained Melissa. Most of her peers agreed.

Accordingly, the following week I told the students it was time to begin being critical readers, and I explained and modeled Peter Elbow's techniques for writing groups. Under this system, they learned to listen and respond by retelling what happened in their minds as they heard each writer read. They also began to treat each other's pieces as text rather than as homework, gradually arguing over such things as intent, tone, diction, and symbolism with a measure of the same seriousness they applied to Dickens and Homer. The assessment they received from their groups also helped the students set individual writing goals. These goals varied widely. Tran wanted to "use a personal voice, but without overdoing it." Amy felt she should "dig deeper to find more meaning and in order to do this, increase [her] vocabulary." Jessica's goal was even more personal: she wanted to "be rid of the tendency to write a piece at the last minute, Sunday night, ten o'clock!"

The project was running smoothly. Students were regularly bringing in self-generated writing; however, I was concerned that they were not challenging themselves to take risks in their writing. The poets were writing poetry, the fiction writers were fictionalizing, and the girl interested in NASA had written four essays extolling our space program. To get them out of their collective rut, I added an additional stipulation. Because one of my goals was to encourage the students to experiment with their writing, I insisted that at some point in the remaining months they write at least five pieces in different forms, such as memoir, report of information, reflection, poetry, short story, and speculation about effects. The only additional information they received was a handout that briefly outlined the elements of different types of writing. Other than that, I advised them to start looking at other students' writing, as well as at magazines, newspapers, and books for inspiration. Predictably, some students grumbled, but the added agenda made me feel a bit more in control.

And so the semester went. As in any other year, the students studied Shakespeare, Remarque, Clarke, and poetry; they also wrote analytical papers, drafted in-class essays, and read outside books. But in addition, portfolio papers came in every week and were filed in folders. Every second week the students reviewed their growing piles and pulled a paper to revise and photocopy for their writing groups. After the groups met, the students chose to refile their pieces or to revise them for the following week. I looked over shoulders, encouraged, pushed, and upon occasion threatened, daring the students to drop their teacher dependency and behave like writers, to produce thoughtful and thought-provoking work. Sometimes I even found time to write and to join a group myself. What I did not do was to read and respond to their work. Because I did not want to bias my reaction to the final evaluation, I avoided reading any of the pieces. But as June drew nearer, I became increasingly nervous that all of this effort had produced very little. I was not convinced that the students could really write well without my direct instruction.

As we reached the final week of class, I gave the students their last portfolio assignment:

Five months ago, I said you were going to collect portfolios and you have done that. The last, and perhaps most important step, is for each of you to select your pieces for evaluation. From your seventeen writings (remember we skipped some weeks), please select three pieces for me to read. You may choose these because they are your favorites, or because they show the breadth of your writing, because they demonstrate a progression in your writing ability, or for any other reason you wish. When you have finished your selection, staple those three on top of the other fourteen, and on a cover sheet write me a letter explaining why you chose these three, and what you think they demonstrate about your writing. Finally, based upon your review of this portfolio, explain your strengths and weaknesses as a writer.

Portfolio Project Evaluation

And there they were. A box full of student writing, papers that had been created, revised, evaluated, and sorted, all without my help. Before I read them, however, I had one last set of questions for the students. Their answers would form part of my evaluation about the effectiveness of portfolios. The questions were:

1. What was the best thing about keeping a portfolio?
2. What were the drawbacks?
3. Did your writing or thinking change over the semester because of keeping a portfolio?
4. What was your attitude towards doing your writing? Did this change? Why?

The students' perceptions of the benefits of portfolios were quite varied. Alex commented that "the best part of keeping a portfolio was being able to refer back to earlier pieces, monitoring my own progress. I could choose certain elements of an older piece and concentrate on emphasizing that or totally blocking it out—try a different style." Brent, on the other hand, enjoyed the freedom of experimenting: "I considered myself (at the beginning of the year) a decent analytical writer, but a real shoddy creative writer. The portfolio has given me a chance to work on my creative writing without having the pressure of getting a good grade on it."

Bridget, meanwhile, felt that the element of time was important, commenting that "sometimes when I glanced back and read one of my essays I would notice mistakes or places to expand my thoughts. Though I did not always have the time to fix what was wrong, it felt good knowing that I could. Consequently, I started seeing my writing as a part of me, a way to express my thoughts and ideas, rather than as a way to get an 'A.' "

With regard to question two, the drawbacks, there was a strong consensus among the students—they had had a hard time creating on a weekly basis. Troy recognized the benefits in the repetition: "Some weeks I had many ideas and some weeks I did not. But it was still good to have to write when I didn't have great ideas, so it balanced out." Jennifer, however, noted a drawback because she felt that "some weeks I didn't have anything to write about and out of desperation I would write some B.S. I wouldn't have fun." Responding to question three and his evolving writing-thinking, Geoff felt that his writing "became a little clearer and crisper, due to having so much practice," and added, "My thinking really changed in two aspects: the first is that I really can take and deal with constructive criticism a lot better than before; the second is that I wrote many philosophy papers which really helped my development as a thinker. I moved myself with my own philosophies."

As the students reflected further about their own writing processes, a number revealed that they had begun to "think like writers." Ryan reported that he was "always looking for things to write on. If I did my paper route and something was different about it, then I'd take note of it and write about it. I also learned to brainstorm and freewrite more." Melissa, however, focused on the importance of her heightened audience awareness, saying, "I began to write for an audience of students, peers, instead of for a teacher. I think that I began to think in terms of what kind of writing the people in my writing group would enjoy. I also began to try to make it the best I could, and be creative, because I figured what was the point of writing an 'outside piece' if it wasn't going to be any good?" Mike agreed, commenting that "I've always liked writing, and haven't really complained when I had to do it. But with a portfolio, I found myself pushing harder to see how my group would react if I wrote different things." Along a different line of thought, Kelly reflected that the demands of writing for her portfolio helped her to "understand writer's block and how hard writing is. I began to respect authors and poets a lot more than before."

Question four, regarding attitude, also yielded some interesting results. After lauding the benefits of the portfolios overall, Susan added that "I gained confidence, which is pretty silly, because all I really did was get a folder and put stuff in it. It's funny how a simple folder labeled "Writer's Portfolio" can give someone confidence in their writing and make her proud to be a writer." Aaron, a student proficient both in writing and procrastinating, revealed that "as time went on I really began to enjoy writing much more. I was enthusiastic while writing. I found that at the end I was having a good time with it. I'm not sure why. I think it is because it was no longer as if I was being forced by some police officer with a grade book pointed at my head."

By the students' own reports, they had learned what it was like to be authors: the pressures of producing on schedule, the butterflies of presenting to an audience, the excitement of trying something new, the satisfaction of reflecting on the completed. And I was pleased with both the depth of their metacognition and the positive quality of their responses.

Teacher's Portfolio Reading

And then it was time to look at the portfolios themselves. I was interested in two things: seeing how much the students took risks in their writing, as well as examining why they chose the pieces they wished me to evaluate. I also hoped to find at least a few pieces of quality writing. If not, I knew it would be hard to justify the use of portfolios.

Of the thirty-seven portfolios, thirty-four had pieces representing six or more different types of writing. Most of the students had experimented with fiction and poetry. Every portfolio contained at least one autobiographical incident, and there were essays of reflection, argument, and speculation.

The students' reasons for choosing the pieces for evaluation were remarkably similar, despite the different types of writings chosen. Most of the students reported that they chose pieces to show a variety of styles. Many also focused on writings whose subject matter was close to their hearts. In fact, the most important insight I gained from reading their cover sheets was that the students almost universally valued writing as a means of examining and defining themselves. Some typical examples of these comments follow below.

> My second piece is a funny, embarrassing remembrance of my past. I love writing about it because it shows how much I've changed over the years.
>
> Tania Shah

Two of the three writings that I chose are poems and the third one is a reflection. One of my strengths in writing is writing what I feel. I love to write poems because I can express myself through them without having to worry about correct format.

Connie Park

From writing this final paper, I began to understand the true intent of everything that I have written from day one.

Abraham Chuang

As I read through this repeated emphasis on the importance of personal feelings, I could not help but reflect on the lack of an outlet for this type of work in my "normal" classroom. And so, if for no other reason than this release of self-exploration, I felt that the portfolios had been of value to the students and certainly worth the effort it had taken to organize and encourage the students to create them.

But the real treat was reading the portfolios themselves. I, who one year earlier had said that portfolios did not work, found myself in the disconcerting position of being so entertained and challenged by the writing that I could not stop reading. The students had not only done more work without teacher interference; they had often done *better* writing. The following three excerpted student pieces—a descriptive essay, an argument, and a poem—illustrate the quality of writing I found in the portfolios.

The Swallows

The swallows were back. I looked up from the box of seedlings I was planting and saw them flashing across the sky. The birds were late—wise birds, for it had been bitterly cold and wet for months; today was the first true spring day and warm for early March. . . . The birds did not have the sky to themselves. Far above them, a plane moved steadily across the sky from east to west, shining as the sun caught it; the drone it made reverberated on the air. At once I imagined myself up there, looking down on the green countryside and the houses that were spread out beneath me like a map. I saw myself, worn-out Seami Kim, in my faded blue gardening clothes, kneeling by the border in the side garden. Feeling slightly giddy, as if from a real descent, I returned to earth. . . .

Seami Kim

The Ratings of Rock and Roll

. . . Parents often don't realize that many heavy metal bands are actually trying to teach the children of America about the harmful and sometimes deadly effects of drugs and alcohol. A prime example is Motley Crue's album, *Dr. Feelgood*. It contains a lesson that can be a valuable learning experience. Except for the last song on side two, it deals solely with drugs and alcohol. If examined individually, these songs are very offensive, but the last song, titled "Time for Change," changes the meaning of the album. It speaks of how all the subjects addressed in the previous songs are harmful. In other words, most of the songs are about drugs, but the album as a whole is combatting substance abuse. . . .

Laura Radley

Realize

Breathing in the warm and wet August air
A night behind in the alley
Between a neatly cut stonewall and a thickly painted
old brown fence.
Sitting on plastic coolers.
Nights never forgotten.
Cold aluminum cans touching motionless lips.
Eyes fixed on the void sky
Or trying to figure out what the hell that thing in the corner is.
A mood strikes as an interval between the
tap dancing
flickered cigarette fireworks
attempts at never really known lyrics
paintings composed with dark streaks of urine
Laughter.
We all pat each other on the back.
To be accepted.

Aaron Thompson

So as I sat at midnight, with the stack of portfolios in front of me, I recognized the writers these students had become and acknowledged what introducing portfolios into the classroom had really accomplished.

1. Portfolios allowed the students to gain a new perspective on their writing because they were able to distance themselves from it. In part, this occurred because portfolios held writing at various stages of completion. They reinforced the concept of writing as a drafting process, as well as helped eliminate "quick trash" and "back pocket" filing techniques.

2. Portfolios gave the students choice. They filed things for later reference; they chose pieces to continue working on. At the end, they finished pieces for grading-publication.

3. They allowed the writers to risk failure without risking their grades; their writing became richer through experimentation.

4. They increased the amount of student writing without substantially increasing teacher workload. Because of this, portfolios removed some of the artificial expectations that every piece of writing must be a "best work" (by tradition, most or all school writing).

5. Used in tandem with writing groups, they created a broader audience than just the teacher.

6. Portfolios also allowed the students to appreciate their own progress, assess their strengths and weaknesses, and set their own goals.

Using portfolios had allowed me to release some control to the students. Through their increased autonomy, they had begun to discover the power of their own writing. And I had found that portfolios, in a word, work.

4 Portfolio Practice in the Middle School: One Teacher's Story

James E. Newkirk
Western Heights Middle School
Hagerstown, Maryland

A writing folder! That's what I needed to create and maintain for each of my one hundred and fifty middle school students, or so I was told. Frankly, upon hearing this piece of news, I thought to myself that, as a middle school English teacher, I had enough to do in my classroom already. I was literally exhausted just trying to complete the normal tasks: covering an ever-growing curriculum, assigning and grading student writing, sharing classic and contemporary literature with students, monitoring the restrooms between classes—the list seemed endless.

The Writing Folder: An Introduction

Despite my reservations, however, and those of other teachers, my school system in Washington County, Maryland, had mandated that all students in middle schools and high schools keep their writing assignments in writing folders. In part, the county was simply enacting in turn what it saw as the new state philosophy regarding writing. The state had decided that, in order to graduate from high school, all students would need to pass a new impromptu writing test, the Maryland Writing Test. The writing folders, even for middle school students, were somehow connected with this new writing test. They were supposed to be part of a system that would track student growth in writing. More specifically, they were designed to accomplish three goals recommended by our secondary English supervisor, Dr. Margaret Trader:

1. Provide a system by which students can see evidence of their own growth in composition-writing

2. Provide a system that documents the implementation of the county sequential listing of composition-writing tasks

3. Provide a system that allows teachers to identify students'
past experience in composition-writing

Because of the extra work involved in managing writing folders, though, I grumbled, if only under my breath. What I saw was management only, form (the folders) and no substance (no uses or curriculum for them). And I felt that—to a certain extent, anyway—the mandate for folders was both intrusive and invasive. I already taught composition, after all. The students were writing in my classroom. I gave them a writing assignment, and they completed all the steps of the writing process (prewriting, drafting, revising, editing, and publishing). After reading their process writing and subjectively grading their compositions with a percentage score, I returned the students' papers. Very quickly the students looked at their grades and threw their work into the nearest trash can at the end of the class period. It was not the best system for learning, but the grades were in my gradebook to legitimize my teaching. It was not the best system for evaluating writing either, but I was comfortable with the process and the results. And I was too overburdened to consider making any changes mandated from on high.

Moreover, as a creature of habit, I found it difficult to change procedures already in place. Consequently, when I (reluctantly) installed the writing folders, I did that and not much else, making sure that in doing so we met the state and county guidelines. In other words, we had the folders, and we kept papers in them, and we stored the folders themselves, but we did not actually use them—except for target practice. Instead of my students throwing their papers in the waste can, they tossed them into the folders, which were themselves tucked into my file cabinets, never to be seen again by the students. They did not seem to want to use the folders in any other ways, and neither did I—at first. But somehow their very presence challenged business as usual in my classes.

This challenge came in many and often subtle forms. For example, more often than not in my conferencing with the students on their latest writing, I needed to refer to one of their earlier pieces where their own writing exemplified the point under discussion. To make this point, I returned to my file cabinet and pulled out the writings from the folders. Underlining a leading statement, I commented, "This sentence really creates a vivid image for the reader." And as students referred to the writing in their folders to help them remember where they had been, they began to see where in their writing they might go. Rhetorical concepts became real as they were illustrated in their own composing. "Yes, I remember that," they noted, or "My closing here is strong."

Gradually it occurred to me that something odd was happening. Why, I thought to myself, should the students have to wait for me to refer to and to retrieve their past writings? Shouldn't they have access to their own writings all the time? If their writings were made available to the students, what impact would that have on their writing development?

In sum, I was beginning to see how folders for storage might introduce ways of learning and portfolios of development. Still, though I could see this conceptually, I could not see the how, practically—how to unlock the folders from the storage cabinet, get them to the students, and get them back to the cabinet without introducing major chaos into the class and diverting the students' attention from the real curriculum. In talking with my colleagues, I discovered that I was not alone; they too wanted to explore ways of using folders, but they were uncertain about how to proceed. So we started talking, not about the what (folders) or about the why (because they might help)—those issues seemed resolved, at least temporarily—but about the how: how next year we could incorporate the writing folder into our daily instruction.

In addition, we talked outside of school to our language arts supervisor. She recommended that we plan for the following year and that we support that planning by taking some formal course work, specifically through the Maryland Writing Project, a six-credit graduate class that promotes the importance of writing in the classroom. (I thought to myself—what a wonderful way to spend my summer vacation! Instead of reading the works of Michener, Ludlum, Steele, and Clancy, I would be reading educational literature.) Despite my apprehensions, I enrolled in the project.

Making Change

At the Maryland Writing Project I read two exceptional books that have changed my instructional philosophy forever and that supported the change to a portfolio method of teaching writing—Nancie Atwell's *In the Middle* (1987) and Lucy Calkins's *Lessons from a Child* (1983). These two authors present specific strategies that will assist any teacher of writing, in any content area, or even any grade level, but these strategies are particularly useful to someone contemplating the use of portfolios.

In *Lessons from a Child,* I identified with the third-grade teacher profiled in the book; she too was resistant to change. She taught writing in what I now call a prehistoric model, one that places more importance on the product than on the process. She focused on isolated skills, teaching those laboriously and acontextually rather than integrating them with composing as the occasion requires. But this teacher changes. As recorded by Calkins, the teacher's transformation is remarkable. She begins to use her students' writing as the basis of instruction that is skill-specific. Thus, if several students are having difficulty creating a lead that is interesting to the reader, the teacher teaches a specific skill lesson on leads, using her students' need for such information as the reason for providing it. Through examples like these, I was beginning to see myself in two ways: as I had been, and as I might become.

In her book, *In the Middle*, Atwell provides complementary insights. One has to do with the way instructional time is allotted. For instance, she advocates using ten-minute mini-skill lessons based on writing problems specific to the students. Furthermore, these lessons are part of a larger curricular framework, what she calls Writer's and Reader's Workshops. The workshops are classroom organizational programs that connect reading and writing and that give students needed "ownership" of what they learn in the classroom. These workshops seemed close in spirit to what I thought my class could become, and I saw too that they would complement portfolios.

Throughout the Maryland Writing Project, then, I kept thinking about the writing folders stored in my file cabinets in the back of my classroom. As the school year began, I decided to make major changes in my design of the class, and the writing folder became the cornerstone of the changes. The changes themselves took three major forms.

First, the students were to exercise appropriate authority over materials and activities in the class, and they were to assume greater responsibility for their work and their learning. In terms of the folders, this meant that they were not only available, but were to be used—and not just stored. Instead, the students were to write in them often; write on topics of their own choosing; keep their writings in the folders; and use writings in progress and completed to help them set goals, look backward, and practice editing. In my students' folders, there slowly appeared a wide variety of writing genres—short stories, personal narratives, plays, and poems. To indicate ownership of the folders, the students were asked to personalize them by monogramming them. They were also asked to assume responsibility for them in the classroom, taking care that pieces were correctly filed and that the folders were safely stored when class ended. And the folders themselves were to be renamed, as portfolios. I changed the name to portfolios because of what it represented: a commitment to writers' development over time.

Second, the writing folder played an integral and planned part in direct classroom instruction, and it became a resource for written material. For example, if I taught a mini-skill writing lesson (based on student need) on the use of transitional words and phrases, I would have my students refer to their own past compositions in the writing folders. The students identified places where they correctly used transitions in their sentences and identified areas where transitions would have added meaning. By integrating writing with instruction, I enabled my students to make "connections" in what they were learning.

Third, I began to work *with* students more systematically as they developed their writing. This meant that I individualized instruction, of course, but also that I started conferencing with the students as a regular part of classroom practice. The aim here was to talk with them about their writing, about particular pieces and strategies and goals, in short to expand and elaborate on the writing process methodology that I had used before. I became more of a coach and a guide, and less of a teacher and an evaluator.

Portfolios, Assessment, and Grading: The Final Piece of the Puzzle

But one piece of the puzzle was still missing—evaluation. I had always understood the importance of process evaluation over product evaluation. And because of the Maryland Writing Test, I had holistically assessed individual pieces of writing with a predetermined scoring guide—a rubric. Neither the holistically assigned score nor the percentage grade I had used earlier seemed responsive to portfolio writing, however. Additionally, because my classroom was student driven, and my students exercised some control over what they read and wrote, it seemed ironic that I, as their teacher, had total authority in their evaluation. If I were truly to change the paradigm for learning through the organization and management of my class, assessment would need to be part of that change.

As I was wrestling with the idea of performance assessment in my classroom, the state of Maryland also was taking a close look at this specific area. The Sondheim Commission, Governor Schaefer's taskforce examining the Maryland public schools, recommended that performance assessment should be an integral part of the learning for Maryland school children. As I considered the implications of this recommendation for my own classroom, I realized that the writings in my students' writing folders would be an excellent source to gauge their performance in writing, and that students' interpretations of those folders could play a role in such an assessment. In other words, instead of my spending hours upon hours, in isolation, tabulating percentage grades at the end of the term, I could work with the student writers to understand their views of the writings, to assess those writings, to set goals with them for the next marking period. In reconceptualizing assessment in this way—as a process involving the participants as well as the examiner—I had found that missing puzzle piece that would support my new paradigm.

I asked my students to rank all pieces of writing they had completed during the marking period. I suggested that they order the pieces from the most effective to the least. Some students had completed as many as ten compositions in the nine-week term and found it difficult to arrange them in sequential order. But other students had no trouble; they knew instinctively which writing pieces flowed across the paper. When the students had completed their rankings, they were asked to choose their three best pieces; these were to provide the introduction to our discussion.

It took one and a half weeks to complete the end-of-term assessment conferences. During that time, the students were either preparing for their own conferences or beginning new pieces of writing for the next term. To begin each conference I relied on the set of questions below.

1. Why did you choose this as your best piece?
2. How did you come up with this topic?
3. How did you feel when you completed this piece?
4. Did you encounter any problems?
5. How did you solve them?
6. Did you complete all the writing goals you set for yourself at the beginning of the term?
7. How well did you accomplish them?
8. If you could have done anything differently, what would it have been?
9. What are your goals for next term?

This assessment conference was much different from the conferencing I had done with my students earlier because my objectives were not the same. Formerly, my goal typically was to guide, advise, and instruct the students so that the particular piece of writing under discussion would be improved. It was my role to be the instructional facilitator for the students. But in terms of the assessment conference, the dialogue was more professional. My objective was not only to assess my students' performance for the term, but also to allow them to have input in making that assessment.

During the first set of conferences, I found that one criterion for assessment could be the match between what the student was trying to accomplish and what she or he felt had been achieved. Accordingly, while revising the curriculum and the assessment procedures, I highlighted the goal-setting activities. I told the students that their grades would be based in part on goals set and achieved as evidenced in the portfolios. Early in any marking period, then, the students are asked to submit and have approved three specific goals that they want to accomplish during the term. As indicated below, examples of these goals range from the generally rhetorical to the surface-specific.

1. Using specific details to support general statements
2. Eliminating unnecessary words
3. Using transitions between sentences and between paragraphs
4. Using more sensory details
5. Capturing the reader's interest by incorporating varied ideas
6. Varying prewriting strategies
7. Using quotation marks correctly
8. Varying the style and structure of sentences

The students seemed able to identify goals, and they appreciated the opportunity to direct their own learning.

As important, I was pleased that together we had created an assessment consistent with the philosophy grounding the curriculum. Even though I had the final vote in the grade that was marked on the report card, the process used to get to that point was a team effort. The students and I generally came to a consensus; there was give-and-take on both sides. By participating with me in the conferences in this manner, the students were taking an active role in their own assessment. We had created the final piece of the puzzle.

Conclusion

To those who would say, "You can't teach an old dog new tricks," I would say, "Humbug!" My transformation did not happen overnight. It did not happen without my rethinking my role in the classroom and my rethinking the students' role in the classroom. It did not happen without some direction from above, from the county and the state. It did not happen without support, from local administrators and from the Maryland Writing Project. It did not happen without glitches, without bugs. It did not happen without the tolerance of my students, who first watched and then worked with me to figure out a better way of learning. But it did happen.

I began as a well-meaning but autocratic instructional leader, and ended as a facilitator in a student-driven classroom. The writing folder began as a storage container where the writing of students was stashed and hidden, and ended as a portfolio that is both instructional resource and focus of writing-student assessment. What I found as I made these changes to a portfolio method of teaching writing is profound: that the students and I could become partners in learning and that learning is what we in school are always about.

References

Atwell, N. 1987. *In the Middle.* Portsmouth, N.H.: Boynton/Cook.

Calkins, L. 1983. *Lessons from a Child.* Portsmouth, N.H.: Heinemann.

5 Portfolios: Process for Students and Teachers

Catherine D'Aoust
Saddleback Valley United School District
Mission Viejo, California

I've never received better writing from my students.

I've never been so in touch with my students' processes as writers!

Now that I've used a portfolio once, I think I know how to do it.

These responses came from a group of teacher researchers after they considered using, then designed, and then implemented portfolios in their English and language arts classes. At the time these projects began, four years ago, portfolios were less well defined than they are today, but even then portfolios were a popular topic in authentic assessment circles. Although little was definitive on portfolios—what they are or how to use them—these teachers were intrigued by the notion of keeping collections of student writing. What follows here, then, is their story, the story of how these teachers supported, questioned, and coaxed each other through their first experiments with portfolios, and the story of how their projects actually worked, from what the portfolios looked like to where they were stored and how they were read.

The teachers first came together as a group in the "Teacher as Researcher" class I teach at the University of California, Irvine, and when they first began to consider using portfolios, they were somewhat dubious about them. For one thing, they were unsure about what the precise purpose of such a project might be. For another, they were concerned about how much work a portfolio collection might entail. In short, these teachers began with skepticism, and with questions. What is a portfolio, after all? What would it look like? Where could it be kept? Why would students want to do this? Would it help teachers at all?

Although each teacher's situation was unique, the questions seemed very similar, so we explored them together. Moreover, the answers to the questions changed, evolving as the students' portfolios became a reality. In other words, the teachers' initial thoughts about why and how to use portfolios were refined and sometimes redefined as their students actually began to use them. Furthermore, like most good teacher researchers, they found that their initial questions were replaced by new questions, which then guided their continued classroom research. The truth is that, in many instances, the answers the teachers sought could only be found in the process of using portfolios and discussing the effects of doing so directly with the students.

In general, however, our experience suggests that considering some basic questions will help ensure the success of portfolio projects. What follows, then, is the set of questions that guided our thinking and the answers that we developed as we went along.

What Is a Portfolio?

The teachers had all heard the term *portfolio,* but they initially had no clear understanding of what it meant in the context of English and language arts classrooms. Most of them had been using writing folders in their classes, but they had a sense that a portfolio is something different from simply a repository for all that a student writes. To them, *portfolio* implied some sort of collection, but what one might look like or how it might function in the language arts classroom was vague.

Drawing upon the model given in fine arts, they noted that a portfolio is a collection of exemplary work, collected over time to illustrate the talents and achievements of an artist. On the basis of this model, they decided that a language arts portfolio might be a collection of writing samples, garnered over time, illustrating exemplary student writing. This portfolio they called an "exemplary portfolio."

Other teachers sought out a different model for their portfolio. They argued that a portfolio ought to contain more than just a student's best writing. These teachers recognized that the fine arts portfolio is sometimes assembled to accompany a résumé and that it is not used as a teaching tool. For these teachers, a major advantage in using portfolios was that they could provide specific examples of writing as process; through portfolio activities, students could discover and learn about their own and each other's writing processes. All that a teacher might want to say about the complexity of the act of finding words to create thought on paper could be made more real through the examples within each student's portfolio.

This second type of portfolio the teachers called a "process portfolio." It could contain completed works, unfinished work, successful texts, texts that were abandoned, ideas for writing—whatever seemed relevant to the purposes of writing. Paradoxically, these teachers recognized that an exemplary piece of writing in this type of portfolio might be a student's least successful attempt at creating a text, for it might be the best example for discussing that student's development as a writer.

Later in this research project, the teachers discovered a third option, namely using *both* process and exemplary portfolios in their classrooms. One teacher had students collect all their writing in the process portfolio, for example, and from that collection, they selected their best writing to create an exemplary portfolio. This teacher used a regular manila folder for the process portfolio and inserted within it a brightly colored folder for the exemplary portfolio. Students then sorted, selected, and rearranged their texts within the two folders as they were written, discussed, and rewritten. In summary, for these teachers and their students, portfolios were collections of writing focused on exemplary work, on development, or on both.

What Is the Purpose of Using a Portfolio?

As these teachers attempted to define what a portfolio is, they discovered that their definitions were linked to questions of purpose. Put simply, the portfolio actually defines itself through its purpose.

In a very general sense, all the teachers were interested in using portfolios for the same purpose: to improve student writing. However, the teachers modified that intention by considering what specific purposes would best suit the needs of their students. Potentially, the purposes seemed endless. For instance, could portfolios improve student writing? Could they be used to measure students' development in writing? Could students use portfolios to discover their own writing processes? Could a portfolio be used as the impetus for interaction in writing groups? Could a portfolio assist students in finding topics for their writing? Could a portfolio trigger students' interest in their own writing? Could one student's portfolio inform and enhance another student's writing?

It is not surprising that the teacher researchers wanted portfolios to achieve all of the outcomes listed above, and more. However, one lesson they learned over time and with experience was that initial work with portfolios should begin simply. For several teachers, their intended goals in using portfolios were so complex and required so many changes in their teaching that the success of the project was diminished. As time went on, we began to appreciate that the mere design of portfolios is a major initial task. Besides, when the initial goals are simple, teachers can work with their students, in process, to develop new, jointly created goals and purposes.

The teachers made the connection between purpose and type of portfolio easily, however. As they selected their initial purposes for using portfolios—to increase fluency or to motivate writers or to enable writers to narrate and direct their own development—they identified quickly the kind of collection they wanted to use. One teacher in the research project, for instance, used exemplary portfolios with her students because her intention was to collect a small sampling of each student's work to pass to the student's next teacher. Another teacher used both process and exemplary portfolios because she wanted her students to learn to discriminate between their best and least effective writings.

Not all teachers could count on their students to be ready to create portfolios that would serve their initial purpose, however, and so they learned to be prepared to change purposes radically midstream. One teacher in an ESL class, for example, found that her students were very frustrated that she did not give the customary immediate feedback on all of their writing. In addition, this group of students had developed little skill in talking about writing with peer groups and did not feel ready to make the kinds of choices that the teacher had planned for them to make. Given these circumstances, the teacher changed her design dramatically. She began responding to all the writings, frequently with grades, and used the portfolio for instructional purposes only: to help students learn to talk about, to compare, and to assess their own writings. Thus their portfolios became both the means and the materials used to teach the language of writing.

Other purposes, beyond those of the classroom proper, also became apparent over time. Portfolios could be used with parents, as a teaching tool, to help them learn about writing processes and writing development and to encourage them to support their children. Portfolios could be used for staff development, much as they were in this project, as teachers share responses to portfolios themselves. Portfolios passed from one student's teacher to the next could enhance placement and inform instruction. Talk about portfolios within a department or between departments could advance writing instruction throughout the school. Ultimately, the portfolio could be used schoolwide to enhance writing-across-the-curriculum.

Who Selects the Writing for the Portfolio?

The question of selection was a very complex one, especially for teachers who were using portfolios that contained only a few "select" pieces of writing. In some ways, this question of selection was, and is, an ownership issue. If the teacher selects a student's best work, that student misses the opportunity to own his or her process and to make judgments about his or her writing. However, many teachers did not see an advantage in asking students to select their best work if it had already been graded by the teacher. They thought that their students would simply trust the teacher's judgment and select the papers with the highest grades. Thus the real question being asked was: Who owns the portfolio? And is joint ownership by both the teacher and the student a possibility?

Not surprisingly, the teachers created different answers to these questions. Some of the teachers reached what they considered a compromise by identifying the types of writing to be included in the exemplary portfolio (for example, narrative, expository) and then allowing students to select this writing from their process portfolios. For another teacher, the answer was that each student should keep a process portfolio filled with ungraded work and then, sometime before the end of a grading period, select from it the writing to be graded. Each student was to consult with the peer response group in making selections, and this teacher found that the students looked more closely at their writing, listened more intently to what people said about their writing, and asked more questions about strategies for making their writing more effective. Yet another teacher asked her students to submit three entries: a process paper (a paper with all the notes, drafts, comments, and so forth), a journal entry, and a paper of their choice (which happened to be poetry, more often than not).

How Can Portfolios Be Used to Help Writers Develop?

The teachers discovered that the most significant distinction between a writing folder and a portfolio is reflection. Reflection is the act of pausing to see oneself as a writer. It creates awareness, a sort of self-consciousness about oneself as a writer. It enables a writer to celebrate her or his strengths as well as identify areas to be developed.

In our portfolio projects, reflection became a part of the cycle of development; students write, pause, reflect, write, reflect, and often write again—over the course of days or weeks or even months. Some of that reflection is focused on individual papers, but often reflection is used to help direct the learner's activities. In this way, the portfolio becomes the means for the teacher in partnership with the student writer to set writing goals that are meaningful to the student and that can be facilitated by the teacher.

Although the teachers considered reflection to be a critical component of using portfolios, they also discovered that it was the most difficult "to teach." The difficulty was that most students lacked a vocabulary enabling reflection. They did not know what to say, and this in spite of the fact that many of these students had experienced a great deal of practice through literature in talking about authors as writers. Although they understood the concepts, students were unable to apply these ideas to themselves as writers. The portfolio, however, provided another literary text, and using their growing collection of writing samples, students began to learn to talk and write about themselves as writers. This was facilitated by having them "revisit" their portfolios for a variety of reasons, which included the following:

Rereading their texts

Finding topics to write about or papers to revise

Organizing the contents either chronologically or from best to least effective

Selecting a text to read to peer writing groups

The teachers also found that, in order to initiate and sustain student reflection, they needed to structure specific questions for the students. Students were asked, therefore, to consider questions like those listed below:

How am I doing on this piece of writing?

Where am I headed in this piece of writing?

How does this piece of writing compare with my other writing?

How did I sustain my interest in writing this piece?

Did talking through my piece of writing help me?

How would I describe my progress as a writer, and what evidence can I give of this through the writing in my portfolio?

Where do I need help as a writer?

If I am experiencing writer's block, what would help?

How can the teacher assist me to become a better writer?

Questions like these helped to focus the students on their own writing behavior. Equally important, the questions were necessary for students to see how they might phrase their own questions when they were ready to abandon the teacher questions and listen to the sounds of their inner scribes.

While all of the teachers asked students to reflect on their processes in composing a text in writing, the time and manner of reflection used by the teachers varied, as might be expected. Some teachers asked students to record these reflections at several points in the process of writing a single text: before, during, and after the writing. Other teachers asked students to make observations between major pieces of writings. In this latter version of reflection, students went back into their portfolios, looked through their accumulated work, and reflected more generally about their development as writers.

In yet another version, one teacher asked her students to staple several sheets of blank paper to the inside left jacket of their portfolios. Then, at various times during the production of text, she directed her students to reflect on their processes in writing. The blank papers in the portfolios thus became a reflection journal. Occasionally these reflections also became the content for their writing groups. Still another teacher had students attach a reflection essay at the completion of each text. This essay greatly assisted her in responding to the student's paper, for besides having the text itself, she had access to a record of the struggles, difficulties, risks, and goals of the writer.

Regardless of the prompt for reflection, teachers came to appreciate the amount of time that it took—time to model reading and evaluating and time to teach students the language of reflection, time for students to talk to each other about their growth as writers, time to write about this development and other writing needs, and the time necessary for rereading and reseeing the collection of writing within the portfolios. The teachers also found that, as students completed these reflecting activities, students' views of themselves changed. They started seeing themselves as real writers.

What Kind of Folder Works Well for Portfolios?

The teachers reported that students initially were intrigued by the idea of collecting their own writings, of keeping them together in one folder. Most of the teachers used manila folders, which came as time went on to have a personality of their own. Through continued use and reference, the folders became personalized; they acquired doodles, drawings, and color. They became worn and frayed, too. Consequently, many of the teachers felt that using a formal "portfolio folder" of the type available in stationery stores would be preferable to using a manila folder. The formal folder, usually 8½ by 11 inches, has pockets that prevent papers from falling out. The difficulty with this folder is that there are no tabs on it, so it is harder for students to find their own portfolios when they are collected with those of their peers.

Other teachers have allowed students to supply their own folders or containers. And still other teachers, in programs elsewhere like the one in Jefferson High School in Lafayette, Indiana, have made the creation of, or simply the decoration of, the folder-package a part of the portfolio itself. Students in these classes created memorable folder-packages: converted record jackets, oversized model cars, even cakes, with portfolio inside!

Where Are the Portfolios Housed, and How Are They Managed?

Issues relating to the location and management of the portfolios pervaded the entire process of the portfolio projects. Some teachers either purchased a new file cabinet or found a drawer in their existing file cabinets, and used a single folder per student to hold student writing. Their students had access to this file drawer, and student work was kept within the file. Most teachers also asked that students be responsible for their own filing. Depending on the activity, students took either a paper or the entire portfolio out of the file drawer and returned it at the end of the period. Teachers found, too, that students had to be taught to do this.

Teachers who did not have access to a file cabinet were more creative. Some of them decorated boxes and kept them on the floor in their classrooms. Some used cartons and crates. Some allowed students to keep their portfolios in their desks or in their binders.

Because teachers were concerned that students might lose their portfolios, most of them encouraged the students to use the portfolios in class and to take home only specific pieces of writing. And in another effort to prevent students from losing their work, teachers turned to duplicating. They asked students to copy pieces of their writing for their writing groups and asked that an additional copy be made for the portfolio. In that way, students kept a copy of their original work, and a second copy was kept in their portfolio.

As the classes developed, the portfolios came more and more to be their focus. Initially, the teachers had thought of the portfolios as an add-on to an already crowded curriculum, but for many of them, the portfolios came to dominate their work with students. Soon file drawers or crates were filled with samples of finished and unfinished writing. Students pulled from and added to these files weekly, if not daily. Students read, reflected on, wrote about, and talked about the contents of their portfolios. Teachers began to identify students' instructional needs on the basis of portfolio writing performances. In other words, through the portfolios and the opportunities they made available, the curriculum became truly student centered.

How Are Portfolios Evaluated?

All of the teachers involved in these projects worked in schools where they had to assign letter grades quarterly or at least at the end of each semester. Naturally, then, they were concerned about how to evaluate the portfolio. Should they simply grade the collected papers? What about the reflection comments included in the portfolio? How could they assess this type of writing? What about each student's process in collecting, reflecting, and drawing upon texts within her or his portfolio? Can this process be evaluated?

As before, teachers answered these questions variously. One teacher whose students maintained both exemplary and process portfolios decided to give grades that reflected her interest in process as well as products. She promoted fluency by giving points for all papers within the process portfolio. She graded all the papers within the exemplary portfolio by using a nine-point rubric. She also gave points for reflection by simply counting the number of entries in their portfolio journals. Her final grade was based on the total of all points.

Other teachers decided to postpone attempting to evaluate their students' use of the portfolio and graded only selected, finished texts. In most cases, they did this by grading each paper individually and then calculating an average grade. Disappointed that their students' writing grades only indirectly reflected the important uses of portfolios in their classrooms, these teachers' choice for evaluating portfolios illustrates the grading dilemmas that portfolios bring about.

What Happens to Portfolios at the End of the Grading Period?

Many teachers simply returned portfolios to the students at the end of the term or semester. Other teachers assigned a culminating writing activity. As an example, students were asked to give themselves a class grade and then to write a letter to the teacher justifying this grade with specific examples of their writing taken from their portfolios. Still another teacher had students create a "special" exemplary portfolio, which contained three or four samples of a student's writing; this portfolio was then passed on to the student's next writing teacher. The students included in it a letter of introduction describing their strengths and needs as a writer in this new classroom. Thus the new teacher met the student through his or her writing!

Now What?

Writing is said to be an act of discovery; through writing, students discover and make meaning. These teacher researchers learned that portfolios stimulate discovery at another level. Through each piece of writing, writers discover something about their thoughts and their relation to words. The portfolio offers an opportunity to marry those discoveries and celebrate a student's evolution as a writer. Portfolios are more than folders; they are a way for writers to meet themselves and shape their writing development. As one teacher noted,

> In the past, I created occasions for students to write and gave strategies for them to improve as writers. From their writing, I made guesses and conjectures about what they had learned. Portfolios have changed my process as a teacher. Students help to diminish my guesswork by showing and telling me what they have learned and how I can help them as writers.

Acknowledgment

I would like here to acknowledge and thank the teachers on this project: Chris Byron, Pat Clark, Sue Ellen Gold, DeeDee Hathcock, Sheila Koff, Mindy Moffett, Jim Shields, and Patty Stewart.

6 Looking into Portfolios

Sandra Murphy
University of California, Davis

Mary Ann Smith
University of California, Berkeley

One of our favorite stories in the folklore of teaching goes like this:

An English teacher slumps out of school late one afternoon, arms heavy with student compositions. He meets a colleague who offers to buy him a beer.

"Can't," says the English teacher. "I have all these papers to correct."

"How do you know there's anything wrong with them?" the colleague asks.

The mischief in this story comes first from the way we talk about what we do. We "correct" or "grade" student writing not so much in pursuit of rightness or wrongness, but in response to a certain expectation. Teachers are supposed to come up with a mark. Because of the way school works, we put ourselves in solitary confinement to give a bundle of papers their due, whether it be comments, grades, points, or even rubber stamps.

In all fairness, we also hope to gather some information for our trouble. But we are not magicians. We can evaluate only what is before us. Missing in the proverbial bundle is evidence of how our students might have improved over time, how they fared in this particular domain compared with another, or how their writing processes vary from assignment to assignment. Also missing is what the students think about progress, domains, or processes. As we sift through a virtual tower of papers, all by different authors, we are limited to learning something about the tower itself and the comparative writing skills of the class in a particular situation. The information we gather, then, is along a vertical line.

The portfolio projects cited in this chapter are supported by the California Assessment Program (CAP).

Consider an alternative. What if we had the opportunity to analyze papers along a horizontal line, several papers from the same student collected over time and in a variety of situations? What could we learn here that we do not learn from the tower? Our focus would change; now it would be primarily on the student instead of on the assignment. Our perspective would change, too; rather than being frozen in time, it would extend to a student's performance across many assignments and occasions for writing. Put more generally, we would move from the finite nature of a single assignment, and the finite picture that assignment and its response give us of a student's performance, to a more complex and dynamic view of a writer's growth provided by many snapshots of performance.

Portfolios offer the dynamic picture that is missing in our opening story. They are, first of all, selections of student writing. Often these selections include the following:

Samples of a variety of different kinds of writing—or strategies for writing

Samples of early work—and later work

Samples that have been written under normal classroom conditions, for example, papers that have evolved as a process

Samples that have been selected and analyzed by student writers

In other words, portfolios—with their various samples of performance—give us profiles of student writers, of teaching, and of curriculum. They can also let us escape the isolation of paper grading.

To illustrate the potential of portfolio assessment, we will draw upon portraits from three California schools. In one, teachers have participated in a writing-across-the-curriculum portfolio project for the past three years. In the other two, English department teachers have developed portfolio projects in English and the humanities for the past two years. In all three, the emphasis is on decision making, that is, teachers deciding on what they want to accomplish with portfolios and how they will accomplish those things. Students, too, make key decisions such as selecting portfolio entries and reflecting on those entries.

By looking inside these California portfolios, we can discover what portfolios in general might show us that traditional assessments do not. In particular, we can use portfolios to guide our inquiries into four topics:

Student writing for different purposes and audiences

Ways that students define and perceive effective writing

Ways that students assess themselves as writers

Teaching and curriculum

The California portfolio examples offer us one other perspective as well. When we look into folders of student writing with the fifty-four teachers who initiated them, we can make some generalizations about portfolio programs themselves. That is where we will end the chapter, with assertions about what it takes to realize the potential of portfolio assessment.

What Can Portfolios Show about Student Writing for Different Purposes and Audiences?

When portfolios are designed to include samples of different kinds of writing, they demonstrate how effectively a student performs in different situations. More specifically, they reveal how well a student uses a given strategy in different writing situations. Let's take an example from a California writing-across-the-curriculum project where the teachers decided to have their students collect writing samples from classes throughout the school—English, ESL, social studies, science, mathematics, and art. Fourteen-year-old Richelle, a student at this inner-city junior high school, shows us that she has a clear sense of drama as she begins her personal-experience writing:

It was Friday after school when I received an invitation to be one of the teenagers to parade in the Flores de Mayo Ball.

But in the same portfolio, her social studies paper, which she describes as "like a book report," begins with the promise of an encyclopedia entry:

Tecumseh was born in March 1768 in Old Piquo, a village near the Mad River in Ohio.

This portfolio highlights, by the presence and absence of dramatization, a technique that Richelle has in her repertoire but cannot yet apply in a range of writing situations. In the traditional grading pattern, it is nearly impossible for us, let alone students, to isolate such a single feature of writing and follow it from paper to paper. Here, in a portfolio "pattern," where papers can be spread out horizontally and discussed, it is possible for teachers and students to isolate a particular strategy or strength and to examine whether it transfers and how it is transformed from one writing task to another. Portfolios make visible what gets lost when students, like teachers, move relentlessly from assignment to assignment.

When portfolios contain different kinds of writing, teachers and students can also analyze variations in the way students treat ideas. Many California students, for example, are from immigrant families and write about what it means to feel different. In the writing that follows, fifteen-year-old Alice uses her own experiences to arrive at a sophisticated insight.

Changes

Ever since I was a child, I have always felt the need to fit in the american crowd. Just to be normal, not asian. Over the years, I slowly began to lose my language as well as my culture. I blamed my parents for not being americans. I didn't want to be the person that stuck out in the crowd. All my friends had blond and brown hair; I had black. I began to only speak english at home. My parents seemed oblivious to the fact that I was losing my heritage.

When I was in the seventh grade, I began my changing process. I seemed to see everything through different eyes. My parents finally forced me to become involved in the vietnamese choir even though I was illiterate. I tried to sing along, memorizing half the words because I couldn't read them. After a long time, I was able to read without having the songs memorized beforehand. Through the choir, I learned how to understand and appreciate my heritage again.

During the time of this transition, I made many sacrifices and decisions. Many people don't realize the advantages of being bilingual until it is to late. I was caught between 2 cultures that were a world apart. The only way I could have both, was by understanding and appreciating my own first.

By itself, this piece demonstrates that when Alice has the opportunity to narrate, she can select and shape details from her own experience to make an idea explicit. Her writing is focused, authoritative, and honest. She has the specifics at hand because they belong to her. But notice what happens when Alice writes about someone else's experience and idea.

Response to BLACK BOY

I think that this statement [". . . that his resistance to the effort made to mold him has been the means of his education"] means that what he knows, he has learned through life experiences. Experience is not something that can be given to you. Through Richard's efforts of refusing to be molded into the "black behavior," he has gained a vast education on human rights. His experiences have enabled him to write a book of his thoughts and fears in hopes that others will be able to understand a different culture as well as way of thinking.

Gone are the details. Gone are the references to specific experiences, either Richard Wright's or her own. Gone is the voice of authority. Certainly Alice's teacher noticed, when the second paper made its gloomy appearance in the stack of like assignments, that it fell short of Alice's performance in other instances. The teacher was not surprised because many young writers have difficulty interpreting ideas from literature. But because the papers showed up together in the portfolio, the teacher—and Alice too—could discover that these two papers, while in different modes, were about an idea Alice knew intimately: reconciling cultures. In addition, the teacher and writer, rather than seeing the papers as two separate ventures, could make connections between the two, noting, for instance, what happens when Alice is asked to work from an idea into experience instead of from experience into an idea. This kind of analysis might encourage Alice to use her own experience in either case, as well as Richard Wright's experience in the interpretive paper. What's more, when connections such as these are visible, Alice can see herself as a writer, solving the problems that writers solve in different contexts.

Portfolios like Alice's, which came from one of the English-humanities portfolio projects, offered the teachers who came together to read and discuss them the opportunity to do more than assign marks. They were able, in this mutual endeavor, to analyze each individual's ability to handle the demands of different kinds of writing and, from that, to come to some agreement about the nature of those demands.

What Can Portfolios Show about Students' Views of Effective Writing?

One loose end in the teaching of writing is the extent to which students can gauge effectiveness in writing. While we have the means to assess the writing itself, it is more difficult for us to know whether the students are consciously aware of what makes a piece of writing successful. In the California portfolio projects, teachers asked students first to select writings for their portfolios. Once the writings were selected, students were asked to justify their choices in a cover letter to the portfolios. From these letters, teachers often solved the mystery of what standards the students actually assimilate from writing instruction. For instance, Stacey understands not only the importance of using details, but also the dilemma.

> My strength as a writer is my descriptive language. I usually write paragraph after paragraph on how a character in my story

> looked, talked, walked and even sleep. That is also a weakness
> of mine.

We recognize Stacey's implicit reference to indiscriminate use of detail, often found in those papers that drag the reader through every moment of the day, from dawn to dark. The value of having students select and reflect on a body of work lies precisely in the opportunity it gives them to recognize and reiterate what they have learned.

Sometimes students reflect on their growing understanding of genre and, by implication, on what it takes to write in that genre. Cheryl has learned the way poetry works: "Poetry, to me, is a way of expressing your feelings without really *telling* them." Such statements can help us learn what students think they know. Then, as teachers, we can rethink what has been taught.

Not to be forgotten is the student for whom the notion of effective writing invites apology. Sometimes these apologies express regret about failing to meet surface requirements: punctuation, capitalization, spelling, and so on.

> I'm not really a good writer except I try to do my best. That's
> why all the writings I do or have done have a lot of mistakes.
> I'm not good at punctuations, sentence structures, and tenses.

In these instances, we learn what students think writing is and what lessons, current or past, they have deemed important.

Many California students, however, see much more to effective writing than merely surface-level proficiency. These students often referred to the writing in their portfolios as "literature." Their use of the term gives us yet another clue as to how some students view—and value—effective writing. It is a term unlikely to appear in any traditional assessment, but in the introductory letters to portfolios that students are proud to present, we have come to expect these references to student writer as author and student writing as literature.

At one of the California high schools, several teachers fostered the ideas of "literature" and "authorship" by encouraging their students to write an "afterword" for each of their papers. The afterword was an opportunity for the authors to explain their intentions in writing the papers. As it turned out, the afterwords, like the introductions to portfolios, provided information about what students view as effective writing. Christina, for example, bills her play, *Pluto's Bar and Grill in Hell,* as "a wonderful, hilarious but fictitious play that I created which features the growing rivalry of two men about a certain lady. Included are metaphors that pertain to real hell itself." The remarkable thing about this inner-city student's afterword is that it mimics the style of an actual play review. It points to features of writing that we recognize as important, features such as humor, conflict, metaphor, and setting.

A final note on this subject. Cheryl reminds us that there are many paths to becoming an effective writer: "My writing is somewhat better this year and I hope to improve it more. I've even bought a thesaurus with over 1300 pages in it!"

What Can Portfolios Show about Students' Assessment of Themselves as Writers?

In the California portfolio programs, students had the opportunity to look horizontally at papers—papers from different time periods and different genres, papers that represented different challenges for them. These students provided us with their own evaluations of themselves as writers, their processes, their insights about what they learned, and their preferences as to what teacher interventions helped or did not help them. Once they had before them the selections they had made, they were invited to reflect on what they saw, as part of their cover letters or as part of their conferences with their teachers.

When Gwen, a young ESL student, wrote a letter to her teachers to introduce her portfolio, she noted progress, but she also noted clear distinctions between her school and home experiences as a writer.

> Dear Readers,
>
> I have learned alot about writing from my english class this year, and I really believe that my writings has improved.
>
> The most helpful lesson I learned was the writing process. Before, I would start writing when the assignment was given, and start on the first idea that pop in my mind, without giving myself a second choice. Now, I learned to take my time and brainstorm and plan my writing.
>
> Although the writing process has helped my, the writings I do in class will never be better, or more interesting that the ones I do at home. Writing on my spare time is to me without pressure of time due, or a bad grade. That was, I feel more comfortable, and my writing would just flow through. . . .
>
> I feel that I would get better grades on my writings if I was writing about subject I am interested in. That way, the assignment won't be boring because it concerns me.
>
> To end this letter I would like to say that I really enjoy writing, and maybe one day, I'll have a career by it.
>
> Sincerely yours,
>
> Gwen

What Gwen clarifies for herself and for us is how she operates as a writer and what she learned about writing as a process. Coupled with the papers that illustrate her analysis, Gwen's commentary dramatizes her need for flexibility in the circumstances surrounding her writing, from time allotment to topic choice.

Portfolios also gave the students an opportunity to analyze how they had changed as writers. At one of the California high schools, English teachers asked students to compare their freshman portfolios with their sophomore portfolios. Monica says, "When I looked at last years writings and this years writings I could see how many more drafts I have. I developed my writings alot further this year." Ron, on the other hand, is disappointed in the ways he has changed.

> My writing style has changed so much within the last year or so! Back then I was so descriptive, with a little humor added to my work to liven things up! But now, I think I'm more serious about what I write and to read it, is like a rainy Sunday morning with no electricity at all while your friends are out. In other words, it's BORING.

Whatever Ron's teacher may have said to him about interesting-to-read writing, Ron has discovered for himself that he has the capacity to be lively or dull. Indeed, his portfolios revealed both generalized voiceless pieces as well as experience and ideas framed in "electric" prose. His metaphor was apt and he pledged, "I'll change my style of writing until it is both pleasing to one's mind as well as to his/her senses." Ron's discovery is a jumping-off place for him to be more than a producer of school assignments and, instead, to take charge of himself as a writer.

Some students in our portfolio programs, of course, were not in charge. In fact, they were more or less dependent on the teacher's view of their writing when they tried to assess themselves as writers. Jeffrey says, "My reason for picking my paper because the grade was good and it was long." These are not the words of a writer, or even of an apprentice. They are the words of a student whose products, and whose judgment of those products, belong to someone else.

Jeffrey notwithstanding, as they reflect on their portfolios, students take on the attitude of evaluators and, more often than not, that of writers. What they offer us in the process is a firsthand view of how they see themselves as writers or, in Jeffrey's case, whether they see themselves as writers at all. And as writers, they teach us what they do, what they want to do, and what they might need from us.

What Can Portfolios Show Us about Teaching and Curriculum?

We found in the California portfolio programs that student reflections, such as the above, offered us information about teaching approaches and classroom or school curriculum. Indeed, the California teachers, in designating their purposes for collecting portfolios, planned to look in some way at what portfolios could show them about their classroom strategies and their writing programs. When they came together to read the portfolios, they had a great deal of data: the range of writing over time; the students' reflective letters; and the conversations they had had with their students, both as the students worked toward the portfolios during the year and as they made their final selections for their portfolios. Kim, for example, submitted a disappointing portfolio and, in her letter, a possible reason. Here she mourns the loss of expressive writing, which had disappeared from the sophomore curriculum at her high school:

> English was harder this year for me and these papers reflect my best work. I enjoy writing and this year descriptive writing wasn't stressed enough for me. Descriptive writing and Personal writing are definitely my strengths. The more constructive writing is harder.

After reading her reflection on her sophomore work, Kim's teachers discussed the dichotomy they had created between the freshman and sophomore curricula, discarding expressive writing in favor of a straight dose of exposition. They decided that the shift was artificial. To reinfuse the sophomore curriculum with some expressive writing would create a bridge to exposition and enliven it, they said. In this way, portfolios can become a vehicle for informing teaching and curriculum.

The same California teachers found little revision in their students' portfolios during the first year of the project. Sometimes the students neglected to include any examples of revision, as they were asked to, and sometimes they included a second or third draft, corrected only slightly for surface errors. Many teachers returned to the classroom to emphasize not only revision, but response as well. When these same teachers systematically analyzed the portfolios at the end of the second year, they found that 71 percent contained evidence of response to writing. Even more interesting, they found that students who received response used it to revise for content and ideas. Portfolios, then, can inspire change in teaching and in learning.

As teachers, when we read and talk together about portfolios, we can revisit our individual assumptions, as well as the goals of the school or department. For example, Nicholas told his teachers, "The reason I took AP English is because I don't like to learn about grammar. It is boring to take apart a sentence and put it back." Here we have the opportunity to thrash out our intentions and where they lead us, what we think we are doing in the classroom with what students say we do. Portfolios can be the basis for informed change, change that emerges from real data rather than from some abstract notion of what works. The approved curriculum, captured in state and district publications, can be tested against our own efforts with our own students and the ways they have responded.

What Is the Potential of Portfolio Assessment?

Although portfolio assessment, in diverse forms and for various purposes, is still emerging, its potential is uniformly rich, and at least some of its implications can be articulated.

1. As the last examples indicate, portfolio assessment is not just an ending, a final exam so to speak. It is also a beginning. If we believe that the learning, teaching, and assessment processes should inform each other in a dynamic and recursive whole, then portfolio assessment can be one tool for making three processes work together.

2. Portfolios give us a new role. No longer are we simply a "teacher as examiner," as Britton (1975) describes it. In a situation where we and our students make the examination of portfolios a *collaborative* venture, portfolios offer us the opportunity to be researchers with a range of data that might tell us what we have accomplished and what we might do next.

3. When our students act as collaborators, we reinforce the notion that real writers evaluate their own efforts. Further, if our students are invited to select and revise their pieces for their portfolios, we are again treating them as writers, rather than as students forced to submit preselected, possibly timed, pieces of writing.

4. In other words, portfolio assessment gives us a chance, as Jim Hahn, a National Writing Project teacher consultant, says, "to put the ball in the student's court" (1985). By shifting responsibility to our students, we ask them to be more than the mere recipients of someone else's paper-and-pencil tests. They must be active, thoughtful participants in the analysis of their own learning.

5. When we use portfolios to encourage students to reflect on their own writing over time, the information they gather belongs to them. And according to assessment critic E. H. Thompson when he paraphrases Vygotsky,

> Only when students are able to detach themselves from the creative task at hand and view their efforts objectively are they in a position to achieve mastery over any cognitive task they are engaged in. This is especially true of writing. After all, when students write something, someone has to make a judgment about its effectiveness. Why not let this "someone" increasingly become the student? (1985, 55)

6. Portfolios can integrate assessment and good practice. When the two complement each other—good practice and assessment both requiring purposeful, contextualized tasks performed in authentic situations—they can serve the learner and the learning.

7. The key is authenticity. As we implied at the beginning of this chapter, school is in many ways an artificial community. Only when we "replicate the challenges and standards of performance that typically face writers, business people, scientists, community leaders, designers, or historians," as assessment authority Grant Wiggins (1989, 703–4) describes exemplary tasks, do we begin to bridge the gap between artificiality and authenticity. Wiggins cites portfolios as a legitimate assessment tool. In our experience, portfolios are also a tool for changing the school community itself. They have the potential to add students to the learning-teaching-assessment process. They have the potential to help us redefine the notion of examination, who examines whom and for what. They have the potential to underscore the growth and development of student writers and, therefore, the growth and development of the kinds of instruction and assessment practices that will support them.

8. A recurring theme in this chapter is that portfolios can give authority for teaching and learning to those who are ultimately responsible for teaching and learning—teachers and students. The packaged and prescribed portfolios that are now emerging from well-known publishers put authority for what is taught and how learning is assessed into the hands of publishers. Similarly, when portfolios are mandated—and increasingly they are as the bandwagon builds—authority for what is taught and how learning is assessed is put into the hands of well-meaning administrators. The potential for abuse, for cementing teaching and learning into a lockstep portfolio system—one system for all teachers

and students—is as great as the potential for allowing portfolios to serve the needs of individual learners and their teachers.

We are advocating, then, that teachers take the lead in developing their own portfolio assessment programs, programs that will inform their efforts to teach writing and their students' efforts to become writers. Teachers and students, rather than test makers, need to be the ones who define the purposes and procedures for the particular portfolio assessment they undertake.

Whenever possible, it is important for teachers, those who choose to, to work together so that they and their students can benefit from mutual discoveries, from conversations about effective approaches in writing and in the teaching of writing. Whenever possible, it is important for students to be partners in the process, including discussions and selections of what should be assessed. And whenever possible, it is important for teachers and students together to report to parents and boards of education on the results of their assessments. Because in the end, what all of us want is more than simply a score or a mark. We want to know what, how, and whether our students are learning and in what ways our practices—both in instruction and in assessment—are helping them to learn.

References

Britton, J. N., T. Burgess, N. Martin, A. McLeod, and H. Rosen. 1975. *The Development of Writing Abilities (11–18)*. London: Macmillan Education Ltd.

Hahn, J. 1985. "Tennis Anyone? Or Whose Paper Is It?" *National Writing Project Newsletter*, p. 5.

Thompson, E. H. 1985. "Self-assessment and the Mastery of Writing." In *Testing in the English Language Arts: Uses and Abuses*, edited by J. Beard and S. McNabb, 55–60. Rochester, Mich.: Michigan Council of Teachers of English.

Wiggins, G. 1989. "A True Test: Toward More Authentic and Equitable Assessment." *Phi Delta Kappan* 70(9):703–13.

7 Portfolio Reflections in Middle and Secondary School Classrooms

Roberta Camp
Educational Testing Service
Princeton, New Jersey

In writing as in other performances, we learn in part by looking back on what we have done. In this sense, looking back—reflecting—on the experience of writing a piece or on the written piece itself is an integral part of our becoming more accomplished writers. Yet the teaching of writing as conducted in many of our schools and classrooms has not often included opportunities for student writers to reflect on their work.

All too frequently, as Brian Johnston has pointed out in his insightful and helpful book (1983, 1–4), we have interrupted the cycle that is necessary for effective learning. At the point in the cycle where students need to reflect on the experience of writing and articulate what they have learned from it, we have traditionally taken from them both the opportunity and the responsibility for reflection by doing it for them. As teachers responding to student work or as outside evaluators, we have told students what *we* see and what *we* value—very often at precisely the point in their learning where they should be discovering what *they* see and what *they* value. In doing so, we have reduced the likelihood that students will use past experiences in writing to shape subsequent experiences. We have eliminated valuable opportunities for students to learn about themselves as writers—and for us to learn about them.

Fortunately, with the introduction of portfolios into our classrooms, we can provide students with opportunities for reflection that have not previously been available. At the very least, as a mere repository for a student's writing, a portfolio is a record of past writing experiences in

---

The work described in this chapter has been supported by the Rockefeller Foundation.

the form of the products resulting from the experiences. Having access to the record makes it possible for both teacher and student to look back at the writing. But a portfolio can be far more than a repository or record. How much more depends in large part on what teachers and students do with the writing they collect for the portfolios and on the roles they assume in relation to the writing—on the procedures they use for looking at writing, what they attend to, how they talk with one another about what they see.

As portfolio programs are introduced into large numbers of classrooms and schools, they will necessarily vary with the student populations, the programs of instruction, and the purposes and views of learning they are designed to serve. Some approaches will value reflection more than others, and the activities used to stimulate reflection will differ from one portfolio program to another. By noting the differences among approaches to portfolios, and to reflection in particular, I believe, and by observing the effects of these approaches on students and teachers, we can enrich our understanding of the potential for learning created by portfolios.

The pages that follow describe an approach to portfolios in which reflection is central. In this approach, the activity of reflecting on and selecting from student work becomes the very process by which portfolios are generated, the driving force behind the creation of portfolios. Like other portfolio approaches, this one arises from a particular environment—in this case, one in which the primary purpose for portfolios is to promote learning, the purpose of assessment is to serve learning, and reflection is seen as essential to learning.

Background: The Environment for Portfolio Development

In the fall of 1986, teachers of writing from several middle schools and high schools in the Pittsburgh School District, the supervisors for language arts and English in the district, and researchers from Harvard Project Zero and Educational Testing Service began to meet monthly to talk about instruction and assessment in writing. We were brought together by Arts PROPEL, a Rockefeller-funded effort to develop assessment closely related to instruction in music, visual arts, and imaginative writing in Grades 6 through 12 in the Pittsburgh public schools.[1]

Teachers, supervisors, and researchers worked together as a team exploring ways of opening up to students the opportunity to engage directly with imaginative writing, particularly poetry and drama. We worked in a cycle of development: the team first designed possible activities, then teachers tried them out with the students in their classrooms, then the team discussed the teachers' experience and the resulting student writing, thereby stimulating a new round of design, tryout, and evaluation. The team first focused on developing sequences of classroom activities that invited students to become perceptive readers and engaged writers of poems and dialogues. As part of these activities, the students began to look back at their own work and reflect on both the choices they had made as writers and the effect of those choices on the pieces written.

The result of our work with these classroom activities was twofold: it was the beginning of an infusion of imaginative writing into the district curriculum and—more to the point here—it prepared the way for portfolios. Through the experience of working together as a team, we learned to think collectively about the relationship of assessment to instruction, a valuable preparation for our exploration of portfolios. Furthermore, the classroom projects themselves fostered a climate conducive to portfolios. To be more specific, they emphasized learning and discovery, making choices and taking risks. They gave students experience with long-term projects requiring sustained interest and effort. They promoted a workshop atmosphere in which students took on an active role in furthering their own learning. And—perhaps most important—they involved students in looking back at their writing and the processes they used in creating it.

It had been clear from the beginning of Arts PROPEL that the team's work would include portfolios. The researchers saw portfolios as a necessary part of the project and a timely response to the changes evident more generally in research on writing and writing instruction. Pittsburgh supervisors looked to portfolios as a natural development for secondary school English and language arts, because folders of student writing were already being collected and not much used in the day-to-day life of the classroom. But it was after nearly two years of designing, trying out, and refining the classroom poetry and drama sequence and intermittently talking about portfolios that we found we were all—teachers, supervisors, and researchers—developing a sense of what portfolios could do for students in Arts PROPEL classrooms. We then knew we were ready for systematic exploration of possible approaches to portfolios.

The third year of the project involved four strands of portfolio exploration. Individual teachers in a few classrooms experimented with a handful of portfolio-related or portfolio-generating activities to find out what might be feasible. Meanwhile, other teachers expanded upon and refined the reflective activities within the classroom projects. The researchers interviewed teachers and students in a number of classrooms to discover more about what students see and value in their writing and what they might be able to see with help from others. Then, at our regular meetings throughout the year, the entire Arts PROPEL team discussed what we had learned so far about reflection and other portfolio-related activities and what we—especially the teachers—wanted portfolios to accomplish.

At the end of the third year we had arrived at an approach to portfolios grounded in what students can see and what they value in their writing and designed to help students assume gradually increased responsibility for their learning about writing. We had begun to realize that what students could learn on the way to creating the portfolios was as important to us as the portfolios themselves. As a result, we thought of portfolios as far more than mere repositories for writing. Arts PROPEL portfolios, we decided, would be generated through a yearlong process in which students would keep all of their writing in folders, then engage in a series of reflective activities. The result of these activities would be the portfolio itself, a smaller selection of writings and reflections providing a portrait of the student as a developing writer.

In the portfolio work of the following year, the fourth year, we further experimented with and refined the activities leading to the creation of portfolios, now observing and discussing the effects of the portfolio-related activities on classroom climate and student learning. During this time, we also looked closely at students' writing folders and portfolios to discover what evidence of students' ability and learning we could see and how we might need to restructure the portfolio activities to yield richer and more interpretable information.

The Arts PROPEL Model: A Portfolio Built on Reflection

From our experience with the poetry and drama sequences and from our experiments with possible portfolio activities, we had learned that the opportunity to look back at their writing was valuable to students' development as writers and to teachers' understanding of their development. Both teachers and researchers had noticed that the reflective activities helped students become aware of strategies and processes they had used in writing. In addition, the activities encouraged the students to develop criteria and standards for their work. But we also knew that the practice of looking back was neither familiar to students nor easy for them. Recognizing that most students have little experience evaluating their own or others' writing, even in the best classrooms, we were not terribly surprised that they came into the school year expecting that the teacher would tell them what was good or not so good in their work, and that their job would be to understand and accept the teacher's judgment.

It seemed to us, therefore, after four years of experimenting and refining, that the first steps toward creating a portfolio would need to engage students in simple and nonthreatening forms of reflection while providing ample support and building a climate of trust. The early stages would involve teacher modeling and oral reflection. Then, as students showed signs of readiness—ownership of their writing, willingness to engage in dialogue about writing—they could be asked to write their reflections on single pieces. Only after they had engaged with these various forms of reflection and with relatively simple forms of selection did we feel they would be prepared to shape the final version of their portfolios.

Introducing Students to Reflection: Modeling and Oral Reflection

In the Arts PROPEL portfolio activities as they have evolved so far, the first weeks of the school year are devoted to getting students accustomed to the idea of reflection. Students are introduced to the practice of keeping their writing in folders—all of their writing, including notes and drafts—and to the practice of looking at their own writing, reading it aloud, and listening to others read from their writing. Much of this oral reflection activity in the first weeks and months involves the teacher in modeling questions that writers and listeners can ask of one another, as well as possible responses that each might give in return.

Questions like "What did you like best about the piece?" or "What in the piece would you like to know more about?" or "What did you most want your reader to get from this piece?" help direct students toward content rather than surface features and toward specific aspects of the writing rather than general observations about the piece or its writer. The circumstances of responding to pieces read aloud rather than looking at written work also encourage students to attend to ideas and their development rather than to mechanics or other surface features. In time, students become relatively confident that they can respond to one another's writing in ways that are informative and thought provoking but seldom if ever hurtful. They are then encouraged to carry their experience with questions and responses into interactions with partners or small groups.

During the time students are practicing oral reflection, the teacher's written responses to the students' writing reinforce the messages they are getting from the classroom interactions. On a sheet of paper attached to the piece of writing, the teacher typically offers comments on only two points: one thing that is done well in the writing, and one thing to focus on in future writing. The point of the response is not to tell the student everything that has been done poorly, or even everything that is done well. By now, the student is beginning to understand that many things can be said about any piece of writing and that no one person—not even a teacher—is necessarily going to say it all. The point is rather to recognize successes, strengths that can be built upon, and to think about next steps that are likely to yield a return for effort expended. The same two points of focus—a strength and a goal—can be incorporated in teachers' conferences with students, both unstructured, informal conferences and more formal ones.

Sometime in about October or November, the teachers look for signs that students have become accustomed to the idea of responding orally to one another's writing and are ready to move on to more demanding forms of reflection. In particular, teachers notice whether students have begun to internalize the focus on strengths and goals, rather than error and correctness, as a way to evaluate their progress in learning to write. They also look at both classroom interactions and students' responses to peer and teacher comments to determine whether students are beginning to see themselves as writers: whether they use vocabulary that indicates ownership over their writing, whether they refer to what they have done in previous pieces and what they might do in future pieces, whether they are willing to redraft a piece of writing that is not working well for them, whether they allow more time for writing assignments because they feel a need to share their work with others and to revise.

In making their decisions about students' assimilation of the first, simple forms of reflection and their readiness to move on to more complex forms, teachers are making a professional judgment based on their observations of students and their awareness of students' responses to oral and written comments on their work. This decision is the first major event in contextualized portfolio assessment—assessment grounded in student reflection and exercised in the direct service of instruction and learning.

The First Written Reflection

When students show these signs of readiness, the Arts PROPEL teachers introduce them to the experience of using writing itself to reflect on their work. Students engage in their first written reflection by answering two, possibly three, questions about a single piece of their writing. The questions echo those they have been using in their oral reflection and the points of focus in the teachers' responses to their writing, but they are somewhat more evaluative:

> What do you like best about this piece of writing?
>
> Which of your writing skills or ideas are you least satisfied with in this piece? Why?

The students answer these questions on a sheet of paper separate from the piece of writing, and they answer them before they receive any written response from the teacher.

The answers give the teacher information about the students' perceptions of their own work, perceptions that the teacher can then take into account in responding to each student's piece. The students' answers to the "Why" portion of the second question are especially valuable because they allow the teacher insight into the students' criteria for writing and into the ways that they apply them to their own writing. In a sense, a student's answers to these questions become the beginning of a shared process of assessment—a dialogue about what the writer, the teacher, and sometimes other students see and value first in a single piece of writing and eventually in multiple pieces of writing.

The sense of evaluation as dialogue between student and teacher is enhanced by activities used to introduce the questions. For example, the teacher may first present the questions accompanied by a piece of student writing from another year or school. Students are asked to generate and then share the answers they would give to the questions, as applied to the sample piece. The teacher encourages students to bring forward a wide variety of answers, then points out the legitimacy of many perspectives in responding to writing. Finally, the teacher presents the answers given by the writer of the piece, explaining that the writer's perspective can be one among many. Students and teacher thus begin to form a community of writers who collectively negotiate the meaning of a piece of writing.

The practice of reflecting on individual pieces of writing is continued for all major writings, both to provide students with ample opportunity to internalize the practice of reflection and to create a frame of reference for the writing when they look back at it later in the year.

Sometimes the same two questions or variations on them are used, sometimes a question specific to the project or assignment is added, or a question that invites students to say what was most important to them in writing a piece.

The questions are not conceptually difficult, but they require a candor that may be challenging to the students, even when they have used them before. If we look at the responses of an eighth-grade student reflecting on an essay she wrote, we find in response to the first question, about what she likes best: "I believe I stick to the topic, and have an interesting way of doing so." For the second question, on skills or ideas she is least satisfied with, we observe this somewhat reluctant response: "maybe show more proof or details." And for the third, on the reason for this perception, we discover a still more reluctant response: "Am not quite proving my point as far as I could go." For this student as for many, the idea that even good writers need to revise, or—more pointedly—that anything in one's own writing might leave room for improvement, is difficult to accept. When she does accept it, however, she opens up new possibilities for learning.

Sometimes the teacher will ask students to respond to one another's writing by using the same questions the writer has used in her own reflections. Usually the teacher requires that each piece of writing receive two such peer evaluations. In these cases, the teacher may become the fourth reader to respond to the paper—after the writer herself, and after the two other students. This practice further emphasizes the sense of community of readers and writers engaging in a sustained dialogue about writing. The fact that the teacher uses the same questions as do the other readers of the paper gives the questions credibility and suggests that the peer evaluations can take their place alongside the teacher's response as part of the classroom conversation about writing.

Students' answers to the questions for a particular assignment are sometimes collected and presented to them as an illustration of the range of perceived "best points" and perceived opportunities for improvement. In the eighth-grade class of the student quoted earlier, for example, the "What do you like best" question evoked responses that were quite varied. For example:

> I like the length of my paper. I sometimes write too much or too little.

> I like the particular examples that I cited, which may not have been cited by other writers.

I like how I was able to change my paper so much from the rough draft.

In answer to the "least satisfied" question, students' responses were equally varied:

I think the way the piece flows is the skill I'm least satisfied with. I think it could have been more smoothly written.

The arrangement of ideas and what I put down wasn't exactly what I thought in my head. It takes away from the writing and what I'm trying to prove, because I assume people know what I'm talking about.

I really didn't have a way to conclude this piece because I couldn't find the right words that would make sense.

From the range of their peers' responses, students can begin to intuit possibilities for looking at writing that they had not themselves envisioned. Their answers to the "Why" question in particular can become the basis for a discussion about the variety of criteria that they have identified collectively and can now use in thinking about other pieces of writing. This process of identifying criteria for good writing is enhanced by posting on blackboard or bulletin board the language that students have used in describing the strengths of their own or others' writing. The posted language then becomes part of the shared discourse of the classroom, a vocabulary enabling students to share in the process of assessment.

The Students' First Written Perceptions of Themselves as Writers: The Writing Inventory

When students have begun to accumulate a body of work in their writing folders, they are encouraged to use writing to think about and describe themselves as writers. The teacher introduces this form of reflection by showing how she herself would apply a series of questions such as these to her own writing:

What kinds of writing have you done in the past?

What do you like to do most in writing?

What do you like to do least?

Where do you get your ideas for writing?

What do you think is important to know about you as a writer?

The teacher might also use examples of answers to the questions given by students from previous years or from other schools. The students then answer the questions themselves, using their writing folders to remind them of past experiences with writing. Their own responses to the questions help students become aware of what they value in writing, what resources they bring to it, and where they sometimes struggle with it. Students' answers may again be collated and used as the basis for comparison and discussion, thus encouraging students to see the diversity of their preferences and of their sources of ideas for writing, and possibly suggesting alternatives they had not considered.

The students' responses to the questions also help the teacher discover much that is not otherwise apparent about their values, experiences, and resources for writing. In response to the question about what he likes to do most, one eighth grader said that he likes to write "descriptive yet funny paragraphs" and that "occasionally I write about serious topics. . . . I enjoy writing narratives." Asked what he likes to do least, the same student said, "I dislike writing explanatory paragraphs and research papers." For the last question, about what is important to know about him as a writer, he brought out the distinction between ideas and dislikes more clearly, indicating that he enjoys writing "easygoing paragraphs" but is not good at writing in-depth paragraphs. The teacher might not be entirely surprised by the student's observations, because the narrative pieces in his folder are more accomplished and show fewer signs of struggle than the explanatory pieces. Indeed, his struggle is experienced by many middle school writers who are challenged to move from narrative to expository writing. But his description of it in his own terms gives the teacher important information about the state of his awareness and about the struggle as he experiences it in his own writing.

The information made available to the teacher through the students' reflections is even more valuable when it reveals less predictable resources and struggles. One tenth-grade student, for example, a student for whom writing is often difficult, indicated in his reflections that brainstorming was the process in writing that he liked most because for him "it's the easiest and most interesting"—an unusual view, since many students find the greatest obstacle in the initial idea-generating phases of writing. He liked proofreading least, he said, because "it takes too long"—and it does take long in his case. The most revealing information, however, came in the student's description of what the teacher should know about him as a writer: "I'll sometimes put a whole variety of ideas at once and take forever to choose one. Once I get an idea I tend to stick with it." This is assessment information that is quite useful to the teacher. "Diagnostic" in the best sense, it allows genuine insight into the student's use of processes and strategies for writing, identifies where he has resources and where he experiences obstacles in writing, and indicates his state of awareness about both his talents and the challenges he faces.

The First Portfolio Selection:
An "Important Piece of Writing"

With sufficient opportunity to reflect on individual pieces of writing and the stimulus of a supportive classroom environment, students in time develop the expectation that they will look back at their writing. Because Arts PROPEL students have easy access to the writing folders where they collect their drafts and finished pieces, they eventually begin to refer with increasing frequency to pieces of writing other than the one they are currently working on. Depending on the intensity of students' experience with writing and reflection, as well as other factors related to learning, this change in awareness may become evident after only a few weeks for high school students or after a few months for middle school students. When it does occur, students are likely to have enough experience in looking at their work and a sufficient body of work to take their first step toward selecting from their folder the writing that will go into the portfolio.

In the Arts PROPEL approach, this first selection is quite open to the students' judgment. At this point in the sequence of reflective activities, students have engaged in a number of discussions about their own, their peers', probably even their teacher's writing. In these discussions they have entertained questions from various perspectives about qualities to be valued in a piece of writing. They have seen and most likely have contributed to the development of a classroom list of qualities for good writing. Now they are asked to exercise their own judgment, drawing on their own evolving set of criteria for writing.

Individual students are asked to select a piece of writing that is important to them and to explain why they have chosen that piece—in effect, to explain why it is important to them. The students are also asked to respond individually to a series of questions enlarging the range of their perceptions about the piece. We sense how these questions work if we look at them in combination with a sample of responses from even a few students. Here are the questions, followed in each case by responses from the same three students appearing in the same order:

Why did you select this particular piece of writing?

"I believe it's my best piece all year. I think it's a very strong piece."

"It's the most thoughtful piece I have written all year."

"I had to use more references to do this writing, and you can see this by how much more details are in it."

What do you see as the special strengths of this paper?

"It shows that I can write a unique piece, different from the rest of the crowd."

"The wording and the form."

"I sense a strong ability to spot details from the text."

What was especially important when you were writing this piece?

"I wanted to write something that would stand out, that people would notice. And it was."

"What I thought friendship was all about."

"My main goal was to defend a thesis with as much information as possible."

What have you learned about writing from your work on this piece?

"I can begin to write something, and end up with something totally different."

"Writing a poem wasn't as hard as it seems."

"I have learned that when you are writing you must always stick to the topic."

If you could go on working on this piece, what would you do?

"I would make it longer, taking off the end, making many more levels of anticipation."

"Be more descriptive."

"I would go into the different ways each of the boys handled their tribes."

What kind of writing would you like to do in the future?

"Short stories, POEMS!"

"Narrative."

"I have always wanted to write *a murder mystery.*"

First of all, the responses are quite varied, even within a single grade level. Secondly, they show students taking responsibility for their selections and using their own criteria—which vary considerably from student to student—in making their selections. What is more interesting, however, is that they suggest that the students individually are beginning to develop a sense of long-term purpose for writing.

The practice of allowing students to make their own selections for the portfolio, and to do so on the basis of their own criteria, is admittedly risky. It requires sustained and thoughtful preparation, and it makes for messy data—portfolios that do not lend themselves to easy categories for evaluation. Nevertheless, it brings significant rewards for student learning: students' ownership of their writing, of the portfolio, of the values they express in making their portfolio selections.

The Second Portfolio Selection: Portfolio Update

Several weeks after students have made their first selections for the portfolio, when their interactions around writing and their written reflections show an increased sense of ownership over their writing and increased confidence in their evaluations of writing, they are asked to select a second set of writings. This time the selection process is more challenging: the students are first asked to select a piece they consider satisfying and one they would describe as unsatisfying. They then say why they describe the first as satisfying and what they learned about themselves as writers from their work and reflection on the piece. For the second piece they are asked to indicate with specific reasons why they consider the piece unsatisfying and how they would revise it if given the opportunity.

Having students select a piece that shows them at something less than their best would no doubt be incompatible with many approaches to portfolios, but in Arts PROPEL classrooms the awareness developed through this selection has been valuable to students' learning. In the suppportive environment established around portfolios by March or April, the opportunity to identify an unsatisfying piece from the several months' work in their folders enables students to discover what they have learned about writing, to see how far they have come, and to acknowledge that some pieces of writing are more successful than others, at least in one respect or another. Selected in combination with the satisfying piece, the unsatisfying piece helps students move beyond the view that one is either a good writer or a poor writer, "good at English" or not. The process challenges them to reflect on what Johnston has called "the *specifics* of their experience" and to break down the kind of global evaluations in which "weaknesses are described as if they apply generally rather than in specific definable situations" and "are located squarely within the self" rather than in the writing (1983, 5–7).

In our experience in Arts PROPEL, students' selections on this occasion show that they are developing their own standards for writing. In many cases, students select as "unsatisfying" a piece they earlier considered one of their best works. With increased experience in writing and reflection, these students have discovered that a piece done some weeks or months ago does not compare well with their current writing, or that their standards are now different from those they held earlier. Other students select a piece that does not quite succeed in some respect that is important for them, even though it received a favorable evaluation from teacher or peers. The following three examples, the first two from twelfth graders and one from an eighth grader, illustrate students' reasons for describing a piece as unsatisfying:

> My grade was fine but I don't feel that I applied myself like I could have.

> I didn't have enough examples and the ones that I did have I didn't express well enough. This was a hard one to write. I didn't enjoy writing this one.

> As I said before, I love describing situations and am very good at it. But in this piece I don't think my skill is all that apparent. Most people think this is one of my best, but I disagree with that. I like my idea, but I think I could express it better.

Students' Reflections on Processes They Use in Writing: The "Biography of a Work"

Having collected a considerable body of writing in their folders and engaged in reflection on numerous occasions, many students—especially high school students—are able in the later months of the school year to reflect on the processes they have used in creating a piece of writing. These students are asked to select a finished piece, along with notes and whatever other writing they have done in generating it, that will illustrate how they go about the process of writing. The students are asked to respond to a series of questions probing various aspects of the processes and strategies they use in writing, how they felt about the piece while they were writing it, and how the process they used in this piece compares with processes used for other pieces of writing.

Students then think about their answers to the questions and on the basis of their answers write up the "story" of how the work was created. This "story"—the "biography of a work"—is then attached to the piece of writing and accompanied by all the notes and drafts that belong to it. Both of the biographies that follow are from a tenth-grade class.

The Biography of a Work

My writing process begins when I think of a good topic sentence for my paper. After my first sentence is written, my pen begins to flow with ideas and words I never knew existed. Everything is written down like one big mess on paper. The ideas are [then] arranged in a mannerly fashion so they make sense. Nothing complicated, just simple ideas in chronological order.

After everything is in some kind of order, I reread the organized ideas and turn them into a rough copy of my paper. Now the proofreading stage takes place. I think of what could be omitted and what could be placed in. I work on my vocabulary to make the details of my paper sound more sophisticated. My rough copy is jam-packed with new ideas and details. I rewrite my rough copy to make it look more organized.

I proofread once more and after everything is perfect, start writing my final copy. While writing my final copy, I see what once were just ideas turn into a paper that I can be proud of. Finally, it's finished! I turn in my paper feeling good about it because I know I did it right.

The Birth of David

While sitting in my room watching *Some Kind of Wonderful*, a movie I highly recommend, the notion of homework came into my mind. Ten-thirty at night is an awful time to start a new English assignment, but I guess you can call it the time of "David's" conception. About half an hour later, my character David came to life as an attractive, inventive, sensitive young man whose hobby was being perpetually cool. After getting his inside and outs generally on paper, I went to a computer thesaurus to look at some unique words to complement David's personality. That was the easiest thing to do. The hardest, as always, was my own faults of writing—the spelling, sentence structure, punctuation. . . . Maybe they're hard because I consider them so trivial. I worked for about 3 nights on the piece, not for that long though. I thought, to make this piece original, I must put in as much of myself as possible.

At last, when I knew that any more detail, dialogue, and sentences would ruin David's secretive nature (totally planned), I gave it my John Hancock and turned it in.

These biographies and the answers to the process questions on which they are based sometimes reveal aspects of the writer's strategies and habits of writing that would not otherwise be apparent to the teacher. The first of the two examples above, for instance, came from a student who writes rapidly and without visible sign of effort. Without the information provided by the student's reflection, the teacher might not have known how much thought the student put into organizing and revising her papers. Even when the revelations in the biographies are less surprising, however, they provide information that helps the teacher direct students toward more effective strategies and processes for writing. This focus on strategies and processes, which Scardamalia and Bereiter (1985) have described as "procedural facilitation," is valuable to students' becoming more accomplished writers.

Creating the Final Version of the Portfolio

Near the end of the year, students are asked to look at the pieces in their portfolios and to review the writing in their writing folders. They then decide which additional piece from their folders they would like to add to the portfolio—the "Student's Free Pick." On a cover sheet attached to the piece and to the reflection that already accompanies it, students indicate their reasons for selection. Some choose a piece they consider especially well written; others choose one that represents their greatest investment of effort; others choose a paper that shows a quality in their writing that is not well illustrated by the other pieces in the portfolio.

To help students think about the pieces that now make up their portfolio selections, they are presented with the following questions or variations on them:

What do you notice about your earlier work?

How do you think your writing has changed?

What do you know now that you did not know before?

At what points did you discover something new about writing?

How do the changes you see in your writing affect the way you see yourself as a writer?

Are there pieces you have changed your mind about—that you liked before, but don't like now, or didn't like before but do like now? If so, which ones? What made you change your mind?

In what ways do you think your reading has influenced your writing?

After students have answered the questions, they write in paragraph form a final reflection indicating how the pieces in the portfolio show evidence that they have grown or changed as writers during the school year. They complete a final table of contents for their portfolio, and another for their folder; the former serves as a guide to the portfolio, and the latter indicates the range of writing from which the portfolio selections have been drawn.

The Arts PROPEL teachers experimenting with the portfolios have developed variations on this final shaping activity, as they have for many of the other portfolio reflections. The first two pieces below are reflections from students in a twelfth-grade class whose teacher brought in writing folders from the students' previous years. The last is the final reflection of a student whose class used the questions and followed the procedures exactly as described above; this student was looking only at writing from the current year.

Student One

As I look through my old written work, I notice that I grew up a great deal since 11th grade. My writing is more easily understood now. Last year I used single words. In this year's work I see that I have been using more complex vocabulary. Even my handwriting has improved since last year. My spelling has improved a great deal. My sentences are better written. Although I still use run-ons, I don't use them as often as before. I never realized it, but looking through my folders, I see that I have improved. I think my style of writing is more mature. The things I write about are not petty things. I think I have grown up a lot in the past year.

Student Two

In 11th grade, it was always hard for me to write a good introduction. I would usually just go right into detail. I wasn't really sure how to write one. I also noticed that I could have used more descriptive words. I used to misspell a lot of words and thought it was a waste to proofread my work. I realize [now] how important proofreading is. When I proofread, I find a lot of mistakes. It is also easier for me to find a good topic, because I concentrate better on my work. That is about the only changes I can see.

Student Three

When I look back at my writing from the beginning of the year I realize that I have changed tremendously as a writer. My earlier work is not as explicit and does not seem like anything I would write now. I have found that this year has made the greatest effect on my writing than any other.

I know now that revising your work adds a great deal to the quality of the piece. If I may quote [my teacher], "Nothing is ever perfect the first time." Each piece of writing we did made me realize more and more things that could make my writing better.

After these changes have been made I find that I look upon myself as a better and more sophisticated writer. At the beginning of this year I thought my ''Lady and the Tiger'' piece was the best I could do. When I look at it now I see a lot of places in which I could change it to make it 100% better. The superb teaching I received made me change my mind about most of my writing selections.

The reading I have done this year has helped me to connect some of the styles of famous authors with styles of my own. This in itself has helped my reading progress. I wish to thank [my teacher] for teaching me the fundamentals of writing, for helping me to become a better writer, and for teaching me to respect my own writing.

The writers of these reflections attend to different qualities in their writing, but each has criteria and standards for writing. What is more important, each expresses ownership over the writing and the process of development evident in it, even though each would describe that development in different terms.

Conclusion

For the students whose reflections have been cited in the pages above, as for many others at all levels of ability in Arts PROPEL classrooms, portfolios have provided occasions to learn about writing as a rich and complex activity and to assume increased responsibility for that learning. The portfolios have done as much as they have for these students in large part because they enabled them, with help from teachers and peers, to look back at their writing and to discover what they see and what they value in it. Portfolios and the yearlong process of generating them have restored these students to the full cycle of learning in which they write, reflect on the experience of writing, articulate what they have learned from it, and go on to new experiences with writing informed by what they have learned.

The approach we have taken in Arts PROPEL portfolios requires considerable attention from teachers and students through the course of the school year, but because it is built around students' selections of and reflections on their writing, it addresses their learning directly. We will continue to work with the reflective activities in Arts PROPEL, refining and enriching them even as we turn the major portion of our efforts toward procedures for evaluating the portfolios. We hope that others designing portfolio programs—teachers, supervisors, and researchers in other schools and districts—will make reflection an integral part of their portfolios, so that the students they serve can also use portfolios to learn about their writing and about their development as writers.

Note

1. The Arts PROPEL team has drawn on the expertise and hard work of a number of teachers, supervisors, and researchers over the years. The Pittsburgh teachers involved in the project include Marilyn Caldwell, Rita Clark, William Cooper, Jane Zachary Gargaro, Jerome Halpern, Rose Haverlack, Lorraine C. Hoag, Kathryn Howard, Diane Hughes, Annette Scott Jordan, Jean Kabbert, Denyse Littles, Daniel M. Macel, Rose McLaughlin, Arla Muha, Joan Neal, Carolyn Olasewere, Cheryl Parshall, Mary Ann Rehm, Elizabeth Sanford, Mary Ann Strachan, Mary Cullinhan Wise, James Wright, Dan Wyse, and Daniel Zygowski. Supervisors include JoAnn Doran, JoAnne T. Eresh, Alice Turner, and Sylvia Wade. Researchers include Roberta Camp and Drew Gitomer from Educational Testing Service, and Steve Seidel, Dennie Palmer Wolf, and Rieneke Zessoules from Harvard Project Zero.

References

Johnston, B. 1983. *Assessing English: Helping Students to Reflect on Their Work.* Philadelphia: Open Court Press.

Scardamalia, M., and C. Bereiter. 1985. "Research on Written Composition." In *Handbook of Research on Teaching* (3rd ed.), edited by M. Wittrock, 708–803. New York: Macmillan.

8 Writing Portfolios in Secondary Schools

David Kneeshaw
East York Education Centre
Toronto, Ontario

In 1977, the Ministry of Education for the Province of Ontario presented English teachers with a new and rather innovative English guideline. Among the many recommendations was one that encouraged teachers to establish writing folders as a support for both instruction and evaluation in the intermediate and senior grades. As a direct consequence of this advice, the East York English Subject Council—an association of English heads and chairpersons from all intermediate and senior schools—met to discuss how we might work together to create a common folder, a portfolio, that could be used throughout our borough.

At about the same time, an informal committee of East York elementary school language arts teachers, in cooperation with the staff at the East York Language Centre, had begun to collaborate on the design of two writing folders for the primary and junior grades. Their plan was to create folders that would support writing in two ways: by providing a place to store the writing and by including, on the folders themselves, printed information on composing processes that the students could refer to when they wrote. In design, the folders also were to serve one additional purpose: to act as a consistent vehicle for moving writing samples systematically from grade to grade.

The blend of plans and aspirations of both groups resulted soon after in a series of writing folders that span the grades from junior kindergarten (children who are four years of age) to Grade 10. Several years later senior high school English heads collaborated in designing the senior writing portfolio, which completed the writing folder series across fifteen years of schooling, from junior kindergarten (J.K.) to the Ontario academic credit year (O.A.C.), Ontario's graduating year. With the addition of this last writing portfolio, even our college-bound graduates would have their own individual collections of their finest writing.

Our experience with folders is now more than a decade long, and we continue to develop and refine the folders. In the pages that follow I will discuss what we have learned to date, with specific reference to the design of the folders, the philosophy underlying that design, the cross-grade communication the folders permit, and the kinds of faculty support that make this systemwide use of folders successful—for teachers and for students.

Folders and Portfolios as Management and Curricular Devices

As indicated below, each folder was designed to be used over a four-year span:

Level I folder	J.K. to Grade 2
Level II folder	Grades 3 to 6
Level III folder	Grades 7 to 10
Level IV senior portfolio	Grades 11 to O.A.C.

Although the design of each folder is distinct, all folders share two common features: first, information printed on the folder itself to inform students about key components of the curriculum (for example, drafting, sharing writing) and, second, a series of pockets that aid teachers in monitoring writers' accomplishments. The information and pockets would be useful as well, we thought, to parents or classroom visitors who could see in a single vehicle both the curriculum and the exhibits the students had created themselves. The one exception to this pocket format is the senior writing portfolio; instead of being a brightly colored folder with three pockets, it is a loose-leaf binder with divider tabs. This design accommodates the three-ring binders that so many high school students prefer for ongoing, daily notes and for storing completed writing assignments.

What is essential to all folders, regardless of design variations, is the service they provide writers: assistance in managing various pieces of writing during a succession of drafts. One pocket or section in each folder is for storing pieces that are still in process, still being written. Students need a place to collect "living pieces" that are being drafted, revised, or edited and proofread. If the writing is still taking shape in any way, then the student benefits from having such writing together in one pocket—for ease of locating.

Writing that is in final draft and ready for a sympathetic reader or informed evaluator is also kept together, in a second pocket. Naturally, even after pieces have been presented for response or evaluation, they should be collected and retained for future reference by the writer.

All writers, including student and professional writers, also have pieces that have been started, but for some reason are in a "holding pattern," and these too are represented in our folders in a third pocket. Such work may have been put aside temporarily or for all eternity, but having a collection point for writing that is in cold storage is beneficial. Students, like professionals, sometimes return to such "abandoned pieces" and begin to rework them after a period of time. The object is to keep them as a part of the cumulative file until that moment of inspiration arrives.

And though not directly relevant to writing instruction per se, one last section of the manila envelope folders (used in the first three levels of schooling) invites the students to talk about their reading: each folder has a generous section where students can record their reading activity. For level I folders, the reading section asks students to list favorite stories. For level II, the list focuses on favorite books, and for level III the focus has shifted to "Books/Authors That Make a Difference." As the folders record development from term to term, then, and as they continue to mark development over several years, they do so both for writing and for reading interests. Accordingly, the writing folder becomes a vehicle for literacy, as well as a place to record writing achievement.

Purposes Served by Ontario Folders

Writing folders, like portfolios in art, photography, modeling, and architecture, speak for the cumulative successes of individuals over a period of time. The finest products are collected and displayed in the folder for both the writer and the audience to see. The folder also serves the artist's need to collect notes, sketches, drafts, revisions, research data, and all the other living evidence of creative thought in action. The folder as collection point gives students control over their ideas and material, enabling them to sort, classify, fix a sequence to ideas, and maintain meaningful patterns in a convenient storage location. Students become better managers of their texts—both those that have been published and those that are in the process of being revised (John-Steiner 1985). In sum, writers working with a variety of pieces of writing simultaneously benefit from reference points that keep different kinds and pieces of writing physically separate from one another and yet in a single location that permits easy retrieval.

As indicated earlier, the folders themselves provide printed information—descriptions of composing processes, along with constant reminders of strategies, procedures, techniques, and operations that apprentice writers need as they work to master their craft. Such information may also include tips on revising, specific skills related to proofreading, or inspirational advice from published authors. Moreover, as we look over the four types of folders, we can see how the writing curriculum becomes more elaborated over time; for example, how revision becomes a more important part of composing in the level II folder, or how proofreading receives greater emphasis even later. The folders at the higher levels are even more complex.

Writing Folder as Teacher's Aid

Writing folders offer teachers a useful observation tool to aid in monitoring student effort and productivity (Graves 1983). With a class of thirty or more students to teach and evaluate, many teachers find that keeping track of any one individual's writing progress is a challenge. Some students may have completed a final draft of a text; others may be on their first draft of the same assignment. When teachers have their students use segmented folders consistently, writing is stored daily in the appropriately labeled segment or pocket. Completed, final draft writing that has undergone a publishing process is stored in the "published" pocket or section of the folder. Such work is ready for teacher evaluation or public display, and teachers know where to find the work without being told. And in the process of locating their work, students learn that one of the writer's responsibilities is to maintain an updated file for teacher monitoring and evaluation.

Work that is still being developed—in the process of being thought through—has its own "work in progress" pocket for storage. Because genuine, deep-structure revision takes time and concentration, students need to keep pieces undergoing this process over a period of days or even weeks. Keeping such work in one place, complete with supporting notes, data, revised or edited drafts, and other paper records of evolving text, is an important function of segmented folders. Until any text reaches final draft form, all supporting materials may provide "second thoughts" for reflecting on a topic. Writing that is truly recursive may need to circle back to its roots, and keeping the roots at hand and intact is made easy through folders. Teachers who understand this process will find that the maintenance of a folder system gives them a window on the ongoing progress of individual pieces.

The last pocket is reserved for two kinds of writing: the cold-storage pieces defined earlier and student-initiated writing. Many of the students do write on their own out of school, so no picture of their composing would be complete without one of these pieces. This third pocket addresses this need. The folder thus facilitates ongoing "snap-shots" of individual writing effort. Various pockets provide places to record different kinds of works, and at the conclusion of a term or year, this tool enables teacher and writer to take a backward glance at the writer's progress over a particular block of time.

Building Links between Grades and Schools

In the East York portfolio system, writing folders move along with the students from grade to grade—a record of each year's writing highlights. Such documentary evidence of growth from one year to the next is beneficial to the teacher as an index of long-range writer development. Students have a section in each folder or portfolio where the outstanding writing of the preceding year is specified. In the appropriate pocket are two or three such pieces—from years immediately preceding the high school years, for example—that provide a vantage point from which the concerned teacher of English can best plan programs that build on previous successes and challenge writers in areas that still need to be developed.

Receiving teachers scan the "finest writing" section to familiarize themselves with the modes or genres that students have experimented with in the preceding years. Mechanical skills or areas of rhetorical weakness will be readily apparent. Some writers will have demonstrated success with the judicious blending of opinion and fact in expository writing; other students' writing may reveal these to be ongoing needs. Teachers moving in the direction of individualizing writing programs will find their goal more realizable with the accumulated evidence that these folders provide.

Moreover, because the students' best writing is on display, receiving teachers are influenced to operate on a "biased for best" evaluation base. Their initial diagnosis of instructional skills achieved and those still needed grows out of a pool of writing samples revealing the best that any student is capable of creating over an extended period of time in favorable writing environments. Time for writers to compose and reflect; ownership of purpose, content, mode, genre, and audience; response from teacher and peers—all of these factors support the kind of quality instruction and assessment we are seeking.

The links between grades help teachers to communicate about programs and to ensure that students experience constant progress in writing. And these links are always under revision. To encourage closer ties in writing goals from elementary school to high school, for instance, this past year the English Subject Council recommended a selection framework to guide students in organizing the material that they would transmit to their Grade 9 teacher of English. Towards the end of their Grade 8 year, students select one of each of the following types of writing from their yearlong collection: exposition, narrative, description, and poetry. Each item should be the student's finest writing sample in that mode. In addition, each sample should include any supporting work such as various drafts, evidence of revision, and editing changes. (Naturally, such texts would already have been assessed by the elementary teacher.) Other writing samples that reflect student-initiated topics, genre, and format may also be included. The four samples provide information and guidance to the high school teachers as they plan instructional units and assignments for incoming students at the beginning of any semester. Thus, with such a clear bridging framework of genre and mode, senior elementary teachers and high school teachers move towards establishing a continuum of expectations and criteria.

The intended outcome of such intergrade and interschool linking is that students will continue to grow and mature as writers throughout a span of years. Students need ongoing challenge and stimulation appropriate to their stages of development as writers. Writing programs that needlessly repeat features of writing, or modes and genres in ways that students have already experienced in preceding grades, frustrate students and impede growth. Alternatively, teachers who lack a solid base of information about students' prior achievement may leave gaps in instruction and skills that students may need addressed if they are to progress in their writing apprenticeship program. In sum, informed planning grows readily out of a system of portfolio samples and writing analysis.

Assessing Signs of Writer Growth

Both teacher and student have a role to play in examining the record of achievement and searching for growth strands (Atwell 1987). Students who have reexamined their folder collections and have reflected upon the contents are on the road to self-knowledge about writer development. They are growing in responsibility as writers and are ready for goal-setting.

Writers mature in proportion to the extent that they have control over the commitment to their writing. When all topics are assigned by the teacher, or when students have little or no say in audience, topic, mode, genre, or purpose for writing, then classroom writing is merely a routine, a kind of charade where students and teachers perform an interlocking ritual. In classrooms where students are expected to maintain a writing folder, however, where they are expected to develop its contents and to build a file of representative pieces of published writing, students view their writing in a more proprietary way. They assume that the writing reflects them as individuals. They relate to the file and they take pride in their accomplishments. With this as a context, goal-setting is a natural outcome. Students review past accomplishments, evaluate successes, and identify areas for growth. Students comment upon types of writing they have experimented with, voices they have attempted, points of view they have developed, situations they have explored, and topics they have presented. They identify what has worked in the past and what could work in the future.

One Grade 9 student, for instance, commented in an evaluation conference that she usually wrote poems, but rarely developed narratives. During the course of this conference, she set as a goal for herself to develop types of writing other than poetry. She was going to begin to explore more impersonal, objective types of writing—not because they were assigned, but because she had come to realize that this was an area she had not attempted on her own before. She was setting her own goals for new horizons in writing. In goal-setting conferences, other students identify language mechanics as an area needing attention: "I need to work on my spelling; my sentences and grammar need work. I'd like help in punctuation. . . ." When writers come to pinpoint the areas that need time and attention, instruction pays double dividends. Learning leads teaching when the learner sets the goals. While teacher goals for the class and for individual writers are important, the linking of teacher and individual student goals brings energy and vitality to the writers' workshop. Teacher and learner are partners in helping the writer grow; and one of the indices of that growth is a folder collection of writing that becomes increasingly larger and more developed.

Cyclical Review and Staff Development

In the world of the classroom, as in the world at large, pressure and persuasion are powerful forces for change. Some people respond to a gentle pull, a kind of welcome aboard to new ideas; other folks respond when pressure is applied and a push from the rear generates appropriate action. East York's Writing Process Course, various workshops, department meetings, and grade planning meetings facilitate change through persuasion. In the various East York schools, such persuasion from superintendents, principals, department heads, chairpersons, and team leaders encouraged teachers to adopt writing folders and modify their courses.

In addition, a cyclical review process assesses the quality of programs, with a view towards sanctioning what is well done and identifying areas for change and improvement where such is apparent. To date, two such reviews within the last seven years have put pressure on schools and teachers to institute specific changes in writing programs. This is obviously a form of gentle yet persistent pressure.

In the current round of cyclical reviews, positive developments in writing have been noted—student enthusiasm, knowledge of the writing process, student ownership of their topics and ideas, attempts at several drafts, and similar accomplishments. Needful change is identified in areas where staff members should alter design or instructional practice. Such areas include striking a balance between teacher-directed and student-initiated writing, employing more effective conferencing strategies, increasing the emphasis on revision, and improving student proofreading and correcting skills. Cyclical review assessments of teacher programming reinforce recommended changes by involving teachers, department heads, school administrators, and system supervisory officers in a network of staff development. Moreover, when a team of fellow English specialists visits an English department and pinpoints necessary changes, the incentive for change undergoes a massive energy surge. Fellow specialists know their subject and recognize good features of courses when they see them. They also recognize what needs improvement, and their judgments are widely respected.

Such gentle but systematic pressure to bring about change leads to program alterations and a drive for heightened staff development. Results include revised courses of study, study sessions on various dimensions of writing, and altered program delivery in the classroom. More teachers have incorporated conference approaches in support of writing, or developed a bank of revision strategies, or reexamined the potential of writing folder contents as a diagnostic tool. Cyclical reviews provide a sharp focus on specific dimensions within English courses. The precision of the focus and the accuracy of observations and recommendations for change motivate both English departments and individual teachers to act.

Conclusion

While systemwide writing folders may be used solely as a vehicle for accumulating system information about writing growth in a particular grade or level (Simmons 1990), the most valuable outcome for such a resource is as a systematic, consistent message to students, parents, and teachers: Student writing matters. Our jurisdiction, fortunately, is prepared to invest time and energy in designing a support for writing, as well as money for distributing that resource to every student in the system. Like paper, booklets, pencils, pens, and word processors, writing folders are invaluable tools that help writers as they work at their craft (Calkins 1986). Writers can and do develop without such support, just as travelers can journey without benefit of modern transportation. However, when such aids make the journey easier and more satisfying, why not use them?

References

Atwell, N. 1987. *In the Middle: Writing, Reading, and Learning with Adolescents.* Upper Montclair, N.J.: Boynton/Cook.

Calkins, L. 1986. *The Art of Teaching Writing.* New York: Heinemann.

Graves, D. 1983. *Writing: Teachers and Children at Work.* New York: Heinemann.

John-Steiner, V. 1985. *Notebooks of the Mind.* New York: Harper & Row.

Simmons, J. 1990. "Portfolios as Large-scale Assessment." *Language Arts* 67(3):262–67.

9 Portfolio Practice and Assessment for Collegiate Basic Writers

Irwin Weiser
Purdue University

As Mina Shaughnessy first pointed out in her seminal *Errors and Expectations* (1977), students in basic writing classes often bring with them defeatist attitudes. Their previous experiences in English classes have convinced them that they cannot write effectively, that their difficulties in expressing themselves in writing and their unfamiliarity with the conventions of standard written English doom them to failure. Naturally, then, when these students are placed in basic writing classes, their "deficiencies" as writers are confirmed, and when they receive low grades on initial assignments, as is often the case, their belief that they cannot write or learn to write is confirmed. Too often, such students, as Shaughnessy points out, both resent and resist their vulnerabilities as writers (7), and further resent and resist doing the writing assigned to them. Then the cycle continues: they miss class often, fail to turn in assignments, or turn in papers that are very short or do not seem to be genuine efforts to fulfill the assignments.

While a portfolio grading system cannot overcome all of the problems of lack of confidence and resistance that students in basic writing classes bring with them, such a system offers significant advantages to both the teacher and the students in such courses. In the following pages, I will discuss how we at Purdue University have used portfolio evaluation to encourage and motivate weak writers. I will draw on the example of the system used in our Developmental Writing Program as a basis for describing how students and teachers benefit, and I will point out how we have attempted to address some of the problems inherent in portfolio evaluation systems.

The Context: Purdue's Developmental Writing Program

Portfolio evaluation was introduced to the Developmental Writing Program at Purdue in 1983, in part because the director and staff felt that grades were being used to motivate and encourage students rather than to serve as indicators of writing ability. Students were receiving high grades on individual papers, and their grades often went up to reflect minor improvement from one paper to the next. At the end of the semester, however, instructors sometimes felt that they had trapped themselves into giving higher grades than the students had earned. This was a particular problem because, after the students had completed developmental writing, they enrolled in the required freshman composition sequence, where a number of them received grades significantly lower than those they had received in developmental writing. No one—students, instructors in the Developmental Writing Program, instructors in freshman composition—was happy with this situation. Students got angry, either at their freshmen composition instructors for grading too harshly, or at their developmental writing instructors for misleading them about their writing abilities, or at both. Instructors in freshman composition had to deal with this anger and resentment and questioned the criteria used by developmental writing teachers. Instructors in developmental writing were frustrated by what they saw as a trap that motivationally based grading led them into.

Our problem, like that of all basic writing teachers, was how to address the problem of inflated grades while maintaining an encouraging, positive atmosphere in developmental writing classes. Portfolio evaluation proved to be an appropriate solution for us. It gave course instructors an opportunity to respond to student writing in progress, to offer suggestions for continued revision as well as praise for improvement, and to suspend the assignment of grades until students had the time to learn, practice, and refine new writing skills.

Instead of grading each of the six to eight completed papers at the time of their submission, instructors now assign a single grade to a portfolio of writing that students submit at the end of the semester. The portfolio contains all of the formal papers the student has written for the course, including the required planning assignments, the drafts that have been read and critiqued by classmates, and the initial revision of each paper that has been read and responded to by the instructor. Towards the end of the semester, students meet individually with their instructor and select four of these papers, which they then extensively revise once more before they submit their portfolios. The portfolio counts for approximately 70 percent of the student's course grade, with the major emphasis of the grade determined on the basis of the four re-revised papers. The remaining 30 percent of the grade is based on the student's participation in class, other class work and shorter assignments, work in the writing lab, and attendance.

Several features of this system bear elaboration. First, while the largest part of the portfolio grade is based on the four selected and re-revised papers, all of the papers must be resubmitted in the portfolio. We require that all of the work be submitted for two reasons. First, we want to make sure that students do not get the idea that they only need to do half of the papers assigned in the course—that they can skip a paper or two because most of their grade will be based on the papers they revise specifically for the portfolio. They understand that only a complete portfolio will be graded, that a portfolio with only four papers is not complete. More important, we want to emphasize that improvement in writing comes from writing frequently and working with that writing. By requiring students to submit all of their work, we hope we are encouraging them to realize that every paper they write contributes to their improvement. We also want them to learn that they will not be equally satisfied with each piece of writing they do. Our goal is to help them see their own development over the course of the semester, not only as they realize how much better they can make an earlier paper by revising it again, but also as they look at the total body of writing they have produced.

A second feature of this system is the emphasis we place on the selection and revision of the main portfolio pieces. The last two weeks of the semester are devoted to a combination of teacher-student conferences and revision workshops. Students come to conferences having tentatively selected pieces they intend to revise further for their portfolios and discuss their choices with their instructor. They are expected to talk about why they have selected particular papers for inclusion and how they intend to improve them. The instructors offer suggestions both about selections and revisions. Much of class time during these two weeks is devoted to revising the selected papers and to reading one another's revisions—the latter a practice throughout the semester—so that writers receive as much advice as possible about their revisions. Our intention is to encourage students to help one another demonstrate the best writing they are capable of doing, to produce portfolios that represent how much they have learned and improved over the course. Thus the emphasis remains positive and motivational.

Third, the portfolio grade is the major but not the exclusive grade for the course. The primary objective of the course is to help students improve their overall writing ability, and thus the grade should reflect how well they write at the end of the term. But one of the assumptions of the course is that writers improve by working with other writers, particularly by reading and discussing work in progress. Therefore, part of the grade is reserved for what falls under the general umbrella of "participation." This includes regular attendance, because much of the class time during the semester is spent in group discussion of one another's writing or in workshop activities. It also includes attending tutorials in the writing lab, where students receive additional individual help from undergraduate tutors specially trained to work with the program.

A fourth point to be made about this system, and one that holds true for other varieties of portfolio evaluation, is that the system is particularly compatible with the goals of a process-oriented writing course. In developmental writing, students complete a written planning assignment for each paper, and then the instructor reads and comments on the plan. The day the planning assignment is returned is a workshop session, during which students can discuss their planning with their instructor and begin a first draft. First drafts are completed out of class, then brought to class for small-group discussion. After receiving suggestions from their classmates, students then revise their first drafts and submit the revisions to their instructor for comments.

By incorporating portfolio evaluation into the program, we are able to increase our emphasis on process, particularly on review and revision. Students confer with their instructors about selecting papers they will revise for the portfolio, and they bring revisions in progress to workshop sessions during the last few weeks of the semester for additional peer review. In this way, students become part of a collaborative community of writers, one which includes the instructor, who is recognized by students to support their efforts to produce a good portfolio. Thus our practice is consistent with what Phelps recently has called the "developmental attitude" toward student texts (1989, 53).

A final point about our system distinguishes it from many others that use portfolios: the portfolios are read and graded only by the students' teacher, not by other instructors or a formal evaluation committee. Our decision to use portfolios grew from a concern about grade inflation, but it was not intended to remove either the responsibility or the authority for grading from the instructors, who, we believe, have the best insight into their course goals and their students' progress. While evaluation by readers other than or in addition to the instructor has value in training teachers to be more effective and consistent graders, and while external evaluation is necessary in programs that use portfolios to determine subsequent placement or exit criteria, these are not the goals in our program. In fact, over the years, we have recognized that portfolios have as much value in supporting the instructional goals of a process-oriented composition course as they do in addressing the difficulties of grading the work of students in basic writing classes. Portfolios have come to serve primarily an instructional purpose and only secondarily an evaluative one.

Advantages to Students

The major advantage of a portfolio evaluation system is that it allows students to put aside, at least temporarily, the paralyzing effect of grades and concentrate instead on improving their writing. As all writing teachers know, when students receive graded papers, the first thing they do is turn to the last page to see what their grade is. For many students, looking at the grade is *all* they do when a paper is returned to them. If they are satisfied with the grade, they see no particular reason to look at marginal or terminal comments. And if, as is the case for many basic writers, the grade is low, they simply find in it confirmation of what they already suspect: they cannot write. The instructor may have written careful, detailed comments, offering specific suggestions for improving the next draft or next paper, but frequently these comments go unread once the students see their grades. A study by Hays and Daiker (1984) suggests that students frequently misread the comments, even to the point of finding criticism in positive comments if the paper has received a low grade. Under a portfolio system, however, students must consider the comments carefully, not only because there is no grade on the paper, but also because the comments provide them with suggestions for improving the paper before it is submitted as part of the portfolio at the end of the course. And because the comments are directed towards improvement, students can read them as advice, not as criticism, as something to prompt further action, not anxiety about a grade.

Indeed, an emphasis on improvement is the second major advantage of our portfolio system. In conventional evaluation schemes, each paper receives a grade, and each grade is factored into the final grade the student receives for the course. Although teachers often modify such schemes by allowing students to revise papers for higher grades, or by dropping the lowest grade, or by weighting the grades of later papers more heavily than earlier ones, these modifications still have the effect of privileging the grade, not the progress or improvement the student has made.

Such evaluation is frequently referred to as *summative*; that is, the grade and the comments that accompany it serve to summarize the student's performance on a discrete task. With a portfolio system, on the other hand, all comments are *formative*; that is, they function as advice and guides to the student for future performance. Comments on each paper not only identify specific strengths and weaknesses of that effort, but also serve to inform the student about how he or she might want to revise that paper and approach later assignments. Of course, many teachers use such comments whenever they evaluate writing, but when the comments are accompanied by a grade, the grade has precedence for the students. They realize that once a paper has been graded, that grade will affect their final course grade, whether they improve on later papers or not. However, when students know that their course grade will be determined primarily by how well they can write at the end of the term, they find greater incentive to improve and greater reason to consider the comments as advice to help them to do so. Such formative assessment thus motivates students to learn to improve their writing and to continue to revise it. In doing so, it underscores the process orientation of our course.

A third advantage of this portfolio system for students is that they are not penalized for an occasional weak paper. As was pointed out earlier, in the version of the portfolio system used at Purdue, students, in consultation with peers and their instructor, decide which papers will form the core of their portfolios and revise those papers extensively. In some other versions of portfolio systems in which all of the student's work for the course is in the portfolio, the work is nevertheless revised before the portfolio is submitted for a grade. In either case, students have the opportunity to revise weak papers before they are assigned grades.

Unlike the comprehensive portfolio, however, the selected portfolio approach acknowledges what all professional writers know: not every effort deserves publication. In a writing course where students are typically assigned six to ten papers, it should not be surprising that some students will find some assignments more difficult than others. Perhaps the topic is not one that the student is prepared to address. Perhaps the student has not attained the skill or knowledge necessary to do well on a particular assignment. Perhaps the assignment assumes a certain kind of experience the student has not had or a developmental maturity the student has not reached. Perhaps, as sometimes happens, the student has done poorly because he or she has tried to do more, has stretched to or beyond his or her limits. If not every paper is to become part of the portfolio and thus part of the grade, such papers can be acknowledged by the teacher and accepted by the student as experiments that failed—but like all failed experiments, ones from which the student learns. Students, in fact, can be encouraged to experiment without fear that an unsuccessful effort will lead to a lower grade. Not only does this ability to take risks benefit motivated students, but it also releases writing apprehensive students from some of their anxiety and encourages them to write without fear of failure. Both stronger and weaker writers are provided risk-free opportunities to attempt more difficult, ambitious writing. Thus, in one more way, portfolio assessment supports the notion that writing is a process involving development, growth, and learning.

A final advantage of a portfolio system becomes apparent towards the end of the course when students meet with instructors to discuss their work and select pieces for further revision. Many basic writing students have problems with writer's block due to their anxiety about making mistakes, sounding foolish, or simply doing poorly. The portfolio, containing all of the planning, drafts, and revisions the student has done, serves as concrete evidence to the student that he or she *can* write. Students are often both surprised and pleased at how much they have written during the semester, and not only do they take pride in the sheer amount of writing they have done, they take pride in the progress they have made. They read their earliest papers with new vision, with a consciousness of what they know now about writing that they did not know before. They realize that they have ideas about improving their work that they did not have and could not articulate early in the term. They have, in short, begun to see themselves, if not as writers, as people who write.

Advantages for Teachers

In a sense, the advantages that portfolio systems offer to teachers are parallel to those they offer students. Perhaps the most significant advantage from the teachers' perspective is that we can separate, at least temporarily, the two frequently conflicting roles assigned us by the institution: evaluator and instructor. Under conventional evaluation systems, the teacher-as-evaluator role is dominant. Teachers and students alike understand that the teacher's job is to read papers, mark errors, comment on strengths and weaknesses, and assign a grade. And it is the grade on each paper that goes into the grade book and is eventually made part of the student's course grade and academic record. The grade becomes all-important in the student's mind, and the teacher is perceived as a grader, more or less benign according to how satisfied the students are with their grades. And of course, with grades come disputes over them—students questioning not only why they received a C instead of a B, but also why they received a C instead of a C+.

Portfolio systems allow instructors to defer grading and thus defer such disputes. In some systems, those in which the portfolio is evaluated by people other than the class instructor (for an example of one such program, see Belanoff and Elbow 1986), the grader role is entirely removed, but even in systems in which ultimately the class instructor assigns a grade for the portfolio, the teacher-as-grader role is secondary to that of teacher-as-instructor or writing coach or professional editor trying to help a writer achieve his or her goal. Another benefit of deferred grading is that teachers no longer feel the very real pressure to write comments that justify or support a grade. Instead, comments on papers can be formative and instructive, offering students advice about specific revisions before the piece is submitted as part of the portfolio and about what the student might wish to concentrate on for the next paper.

A portfolio system also allows teachers to emphasize progress in writing in a way that is more difficult in conventionally evaluated courses. When even the first papers in a course are graded, everything the student writes counts toward the summative final grade. This kind of grading is problematic because the written text as an evaluated product can be assessed by a large number of overlapping criteria. Writing is not like math: in math, students can get good grades by mastering discrete skills necessary to get the correct answers to easy problems early in the course and can learn additional skills that will enable them to do more complex problems correctly later. The difficult problems are assigned after the students have studied the concepts necessary to solve them. But in writing, all of the complexities of planning and developing and expressing one's ideas are present in every writing task. There are no "easy problems" in writing, especially for the basic writer. Writing can go wrong in numerous ways. Teachers feel the frustration of not being able to teach everything before they grade, of wishing that their students knew at the beginning of the course what they will know at the end. They see errors and weaknesses that they know will be addressed later in the term and must decide whether to overlook them at first or to base early grades on different or fewer criteria than they will at the end.

Portfolio systems allow teachers to address this problem by withholding the assigning of grades until the end of the course, and thus they can more easily focus the course on writing as a learnable craft rather than as a talent or a static skill. They need not worry that, because they have not addressed a particular concept, students will not be able to write well. The emphasis is on an accumulation of writing abilities, not on those the student brings to the class.

Moreover, in basic writing classes, the deferral of grades is particularly useful because basic writers, by definition, are likely to do poorly on early papers. They will have problems not only with development, organization, and coherence, but also with syntax, diction, and grammar. Portfolio evaluation provides these students with the time they need to gain control over these problems, to learn to detect error patterns, and to correct them during revision. Their final products—and their final grades—will thus reflect the abilities they have developed over the semester.

Problems of Portfolio Systems

It is tempting to dwell on the advantages that portfolio evaluation systems have over conventional approaches of evaluating writing. Especially from a teacher's point of view, eliminating or at least deferring grades places the emphasis of a course on helping students learn and improve rather than on rating their performance. However, there are several problems that programs or individual teachers planning to implement a portfolio system must consider.

First, the educational system with which students are familiar places great importance on grades as indices of performance. Students have learned to rely on grades to motivate, threaten, or reassure them. They think in terms of grade-point averages, of eligibility to participate in athletics or social organizations, of financial aid, of getting good jobs. Many, if not most, students will feel insecure about their performance and progress without the security blanket—or threat—that grades provide. This is true not only of basic writers, for whom grades have generally meant failure, but also of good writers who have relied on grades for motivation and reward.

Teachers can address this grade dependency and the anxiety it produces in several ways. One of the most important is to make the comments on the papers as clear and specific as possible. It may be possible to faintly praise or mildly criticize a paper if the comments are accompanied by a grade. The C− lets the student know what the language really means. But without a grade at the end of the paper, comments must tell the student precisely what is good and what is bad about each paper and what the student should consider both before revising it and while writing the next paper. The comments serve an important *instructional* purpose; they are not simply justifications for the grade, and students will need to use the comments to guide them as they prepare their portfolio revisions. Thus an important part of teacher training in programs that use portfolio evaluation is the discussion of sample student writing and the kinds of comments that will be most helpful to the student who reads them. Such comments for us are a combination of genuine reader responses to the content and development of the paper, of questions about what is unclear or confusing, of suggestions for changes, and of praise for what is successful and explanation of what, for that reader at least, is not.

Offering to assign a tentative grade to one paper of the student's choosing during the first half of the course also helps to relieve anxiety about grades, although students must know that the grade will not be recorded and is not binding. Interestingly enough, when I and other teachers in our program have made this offer, we have few takers. Perhaps knowing that they can have a tentative grade if they want one is sufficient to help students overcome anxiety about their performance, although they are just as likely to read comments carefully enough to know what the instructor thinks of their work.

Another particularly useful strategy is to hold midterm conferences with individual students to discuss their performance and progress in detail and to give them a tentative, nonbinding grade at that time. Not only can such conferences help teachers sense whether students are misinterpreting comments or overestimating their performance, but they give teachers an opportunity to show students the criteria by which their final portfolios will be evaluated. And even an explicitly nonbinding grade is useful in letting students know where they stand at the moment and in relieving teachers from the concern that some students may not have a clear sense of whether they are doing well. This is also an appropriate time to counsel students who are in danger of failing to consider withdrawing from the course if they choose, as well as to encourage those who show promise but whose work is marginal.

Because the goal of our Developmental Writing Program is to introduce students to composing process strategies and promote a general ability to write effectively, the selected portfolio system we use is appropriate. However, in curricula where each assignment is designed to teach a specific skill or strategy, basing most of the student's grade on a selected portfolio may seem inappropriate. For example, the second semester freshman composition course at Purdue focuses on varieties of academic writing. Students write a report, a book or film or article review, an essay examination response, a proposal, a research paper, and so on. Other writing courses may have students write a certain number of papers with a specific aim or in a certain genre.

In such cases, the question arises about the importance of each kind of writing and the fairness of basing grades on what may be a selection that does not represent the range of abilities students are expected to develop. While it is possible to avoid this problem by requiring students to submit comprehensive portfolios and grading each paper, such a solution is only partly satisfactory. In the first place, students find it difficult to revise each of their papers, rather than several selected pieces, during the last few weeks of the semester, which is usually their busiest, most pressured time. Because it is unlikely that they will be able to devote the necessary time to revising each paper, their portfolio may not accurately reflect how well they can write. In the second place, rereading a full semester's work is an unreasonable burden for the teacher. Finally, having the course grade depend on all of the papers contradicts one of the advantages of the portfolio system discussed earlier: students are not penalized for an occasional weak paper or led to believe that every effort to write ends in success.

A more satisfactory solution to this problem, and one that is consistent with the notion that a portfolio is a *selection* of work, is to establish at the outset of the course specific distribution requirements. Perhaps students will be required to revise a certain number of papers from each half of the course or to include one representative paper for each "discrete" skill, genre, or aim. Belanoff and Elbow describe one such program at SUNY–Stony Brook in which portfolios consist of one narrative, descriptive, or expressive piece, one "formal" essay, one analysis of a prose text, and one additional "piece of in-class writing done without the benefit of feedback of revising" (1986, 27).

One group of freshman composition instructors at Purdue is addressing this problem in another way. Their students submit portfolios for evaluation during the semester, once after they have written expressive papers and once after they have written persuasive papers.

The students' portfolios are evaluated each time so that students receive grades for each discourse type they have practiced. Students' final course grades are composites of the two portfolio grades plus attendance, participation, and so on.

Conclusion

Over the past two decades, writing instruction has changed from an emphasis on the written product to an emphasis on the writing process. We have stopped simply assigning papers, waiting for them to be submitted, grading and returning them. Instead, we teach our students strategies for planning, drafting, revising, and editing their work, recognizing that the practice of these overlapping parts of the writing process enables students to produce better final papers. We no longer assume that good writers are people capable of producing polished work on their first try; we know that writers do not often "get it right" the first time.

Portfolio assessment is a natural extension of our emphasis on process, reflecting that writing can always be made better and that writers can always improve. In particular, portfolio systems of evaluation remove the often punitive element that comes from grading work before students have practiced and begun to master the composing process. For that reason, portfolio evaluation is not only consistent with current theories about how people write, but is particularly appropriate for basic writing classes. Basic writers, as Mike Rose has so eloquently shown us in his recent *Lives on the Boundary* (1989), need the opportunity to see themselves as people who can learn and improve. They need to see teachers as collaborators in their learning and supporters of it, not simply as judges of their weaknesses. Portfolio evaluation supports this positive, collaborative view of education.

References

Belanoff, P., and P. Elbow. 1986. "Using Portfolios to Increase Collaboration and Community in a Writing Program." *WPA: Writing Program Administration* 9:27–40.

Hays, M. F., and D. A. Daiker. 1984. "Using Protocol Analysis in Evaluating Responses to Student Writing." *Freshman English News* 13:1–4, 10.

Phelps, L. W. 1989. "Images of Student Writing: The Deep Structure of Teacher Response." In *Writing and Responding,* edited by C. Anson, 37–67. Urbana, Ill.: National Council of Teachers of English.

Rose, M. 1989. *Lives on the Boundary: The Struggles and Achievements of America's Underprepared.* New York: The Free Press.

Shaughnessy, M. P. 1977. *Errors and Expectations.* New York: Oxford.

10 Portfolios in the Writing Classroom: A Final Reflection

Kathleen Blake Yancey
University of North Carolina at Charlotte

During the last twenty years, the field of writing assessment has changed in ways both dramatic and profound. As Catharine Lucas has clearly shown, there has been a tremendous shift—from objectively based, empiricist methods of evaluating writing to ones more contextually situated, more rhetorically defined, more process oriented (1988, 4–5). One pedagogical and assessment tool that has facilitated this shift is the portfolio.

Portfolio work in the field of composition studies is recent enough, having started formally some twelve years ago, but the idea of a portfolio is not new. Artists, for instance, have long collected their best works in portfolios for various purposes: to complete course work, to request an exhibition, to seek employment. Musicians likewise gather and assemble their scores into portfolio collections. In the financial world, portfolios signify both wealth and status, indicating that the portfolio builder has sufficient capital to investigate ways and places to invest it. Also vested with status, ministers of state arrive at their posts with portfolios in hand. Another, more commercial manifestation of "portfolio" has appeared just lately in several magazines: *USAir Magazine*, with its regular "Folio" section showcasing an artistic talent, for example; in Marriott Hotel's magazine *Portfolio*; and in *Indiana Arts*, with its regular "Portfolio" feature, which introduces artists and their work.

Characteristics of Portfolios

Regardless of the particular context, however, all of these portfolios, like portfolios used in writing classes, share three essential characteristics. They are, first, longitudinal in nature; second, diverse in content; and third, almost always collaborative in ownership and composition. A summary consideration of the nature and function of the artist's and the financier's portfolios elucidates these shared features.

Whether for class or for work, the artist's portfolio is intended to demonstrate growth, to show development over time from early to later work. Typically, this portfolio shows a range of performance by way of pieces and projects reflecting stylistic and thematic interests of various sorts and composed in various media, one in charcoal perhaps, another in watercolors. It is therefore unlikely that an artist would assemble a portfolio focused solely on still lifes, or one constituted strictly by Carolinian landscapes. Rather, the artist might include one example of each, in addition to examples of other types, a sketch perhaps or a project of another type. In other words, the intent of an artist's portfolio is to show range *in talent* and *in time*. As important is the way the portfolio is created, with the assistance of others. As artists develop, they benefit in both acknowledged and unspoken ways from teacher commentary, from peer critique, from collegial discussion. Pieces in the portfolio may have been shaped and reseen in response to specific recommendations from others. And the artists may have consulted still others in deciding which pieces best exemplify their performance.

Financial portfolios are defined by the same features. Typically, their aim is to show growth, which in this case means to produce capital. Long-term growth is therefore the intended purpose of these portfolios. To accomplish this goal, financiers create portfolios that are diverse, that contain various kinds of financial instruments—bonds, mutual funds, stocks, and the like—the theory being that if one instrument fails, the others will compensate for it. The sum of these portfolios is greater than the parts. And like artists' portfolios, financial portfolios are created by any number of people: by those who have the money to invest; by professional financial planners who are paid to contribute their time and expertise to the project, possibly at regular intervals; by other experts; and by nonexperts such as friends and colleagues.

Portfolios in writing classes, the focus of both this discussion and this volume, share these characteristics. Like their counterparts in these other areas, writing portfolios often have several intents, first among them to document the development and maturity of students' writing. In a portfolio classroom, the teacher sets out quite explicitly to "create" the time necessary for writers to develop. In practice, what this means is that the piece initiated on Monday need not be submitted a week or two later for a final evaluation. Instead, it can be reseen and reshaped and revised in light of what is learned days or weeks or even a month or two later. Moreover, as a "system," the portfolio is open rather than closed. Its contents are intended to be diverse and inclusive: expressionistic, transactional, poetic, fragmented, and polished alike. The assumption is that all these pieces speak in some ways to the processes of writing managed, or even just attempted, by their composer. The writer is invited to try new ways of seeing, new methods of development, new voices. And finally, the portfolio is created collaboratively: by the student as author, working with the teacher and other students as partners, who respond to and advise the writer, helping to evaluate and rework and select pieces to be submitted for the institutional assessment that finally determines the grade.

Portfolios in Writing Classrooms

In addition to these characteristics, however, portfolios in composition classes often exhibit one other defining characteristic: they include some metacognitive work, that is, some exploration by the writers of their own composing processes and of their own development as writers. These explorations can involve thinking, describing, analysis, and commentary, and they can include summaries of the writers' feelings about successful and unsuccessful writings and about teacher-identified and author-identified composing goals. The purposes of such explorations are numerous and diverse:

> To nurture a self-reflexiveness about writing
>
> To provide information about what is going on "within" the writers to help them set their own agendas and thus exercise some control over their own development in appropriate ways
>
> To help students begin to think about writers generally and what they do
>
> To nurture the identity of writer in the students
>
> To help the writers think about and articulate their response to their own writing and to see it longitudinally, to see it as the story of their development as thinkers and writers, as creators and composers
>
> To invite the writers to compose narratives of their own development
>
> To see their own writings separately and then together, in context

In Kenneth Burke's language, the portfolio acts as a frame, a terministic screen enabling new insights, ones that are less likely and sometimes impossible without the frame. Because there is a frame, a folder, the pieces within it are assumed to have a relationship, but it is a relationship that the writer-reader perceives and establishes. At the least, the pieces always speak to ways that the writer is becoming. But these pieces can tell much more, as writers explore what the relationships among the pieces may be and which composing processes may be appropriate for different rhetorical situations. In sum, what this portfolio frame means is that through it students are more likely to see their work and themselves in new ways—precisely because the portfolio invites both perception and discussion of relationships among pieces, of threads common to diverse pieces, and of ways that writers compose.

Writing portfolios within the classroom are thus paradoxical. On the one hand, they are quite simple: a mere pedagogical tool with assessment capability. On the other hand, writing portfolios promise to change significantly what goes on in writing classrooms—because of the messages they send, the authority they assign, the ways they motivate students, and the insights they challenge students to perceive and articulate. As important, these mere collections, or folders, can emphasize and extend in new ways other processes, particularly when it comes time to respond to and evaluate students' work.

For some time now, writing classrooms have been about writing, not about products. Instead of teaching writing solely through examination of text, teachers invite students to learn how to write by writing: to compose with their colleagues, to collaborate in workshops and in peer groups, to learn methods of planning and invention, to share their writing with others, to learn both conceptually and experientially about the notion of discourse community as they explore the worlds of private and public discourse. Unfortunately, however, what often happens at the point when students submit their work formally and when "evaluation" comes into play is a return to a product-based methodology. It is at this point in the pedagogy that process and becoming are lost.

What seems to happen is this. Teachers assign papers and set appropriate due dates; and within the allotted time, writers are given many opportunities to draft and redraft. But at the moment when papers are submitted for evaluation, two major backward moves occur. The first move is that the interpretive transaction among writer and reader and text is shut down, perhaps in part because of the nature of evaluation, true enough, but also in part as a function of the power and finality of the grade. As Nancy Sommers (1982) has shown, final product-based evaluations have a chilling effect on reader-writer transactions. When graded, student writing is reduced to a mere vehicle conveying a grade, not an opportunity for further discussion. Consequently, the likelihood that a graded piece will motivate students to continue what Sharon Crowley has called a continuing conversation about writing is diminished (1989, 31–48).

The second backward move involves the context in which student work is read. In traditional classrooms, essays are not ordinarily read in the context of the past, that is, in the context of the student's own work, but rather in the context of the collective present, that is, in the context of all responses to a particular assignment. Put simply, teachers sit down with the proverbial stack of papers and read them to see how students did on a particular assignment. Teachers read to see how the students did (how the assignment functioned) and how the students responded to the assignment (how they did on it). Only secondarily are students' essays read relative to the authors' growth in writing, if at all. The papers of weaker writers are thus always compared with those of stronger writers, rarely to work of their own; they remain locked at the lower end of the scale, their growth and improvement invisible, both to the teachers and to themselves.

The portfolio prevents these backward moves as it extends current practice. In portfolio-based writing classes, individual assignments may be submitted and graded comparatively and individually as in "regular" classes. But when student work is ultimately submitted within the context of a portfolio, the same assignment is read relative to the context of each author's own development. In the final analysis—when the portfolio itself is graded—some assignments may not be included, may not even "count" for the grade. They do "count," however, in the formative sense, in the development of the writer, and that too is what the portfolio is about. These pieces may not "work," or they may be only fragmentary, but together all the pieces make the puzzle, just as all these pieces compose the writer. Within the portfolio, fragments can count institutionally as well as part of the course-long continuing conversations between the authors and their audiences.

In portfolio-based writing classes, then, the reader-writer-text transaction invoked by each piece is conducted within the larger context provided by all the pieces. A writer's pieces are not seen so much in isolation or relative to others' pieces, but rather relative to the writer's own development as represented in the portfolio. Furthermore, until the final portfolio's submission, the writer has an opportunity to comment upon any piece, to see it in new ways, and thereby to recontextualize it and to help direct her or his own learning. Moreover, in order to see and comment, to continue the transaction, and to include it in the larger conversation, the writer needs to read and consider the teacher's reading of each piece. Eventually, of course, portfolios are submitted, and closure occurs. But premature closure, at least, has been deferred, and in the interim an interest in how the writer could develop has provided a chief motive for teacher and student reading and writing.

Principles of Portfolio Practice

Culturally, portfolios thus are seen to have common characteristics, and writing portfolios per se also are seen to nurture metacognition and to enact response and assessment consistent with the transactional meaning-making nature of reading and writing. As important, although the work in portfolios is still exploratory, certain principles guiding classroom portfolio practice are evolving. First, portfolio programs seem to work best when teacher participation in them is voluntary. Second, teachers need to design their own portfolio projects relative to their own curricular demands and concerns. Third, given the distinction between formative and summative evaluation, teachers need to read student work differently according to how complete the portfolio is. Fourth, portfolio participants should expect the portfolios to provide benefits in addition to the ones described already. And fifth, teachers should expect to revise their approach to portfolios continually on the basis of their experience with them. These principles deserve some brief elaboration here as they all appear in the chapters leading to this one.

Grass-Roots, Voluntary Adoption

In general, portfolios have become increasingly well known within composition studies because of teacher enthusiasm. Portfolios are a grass-roots phenomenon, a practice that teachers, not legislators or administrators, have introduced. (Vermont and Maryland stand as two well-known exceptions.) But one of the reasons that the teachers who have tried portfolios are so positive about them is that they have been able to exercise control over them; that is, the teachers decide whether to use portfolios, help define their uses, include them in curricula in appropriate ways, and revise them on the basis of their own and others' experience.

In other words, portfolio projects work well when designed and staffed by volunteers, and they are attracting attention and becoming more widespread not because they are mandated, but because the teachers who do use them are the best recruiters. Their behavior and attitude invite others to join. It is almost axiomatic among portfolio practitioners that voluntary participation is about the only kind worth having, particularly since portfolios require specific planning, different reading processes, and more time for reading. The first guiding principle for portfolio practice is, then, that teachers who try portfolios should want to do so.

Context-Specific Design

A second guiding principle has to do with the nature of portfolio projects: they are not portable. What this means is that teachers who consider using portfolios need to do so within the context of their own academic situation. This context will help the teachers determine the purposes the portfolios will serve: curricular purposes, like helping students learn to write letters of application, occasional essays, term papers, lab reports, or poetry—or to learn a bit about all of these. Sometimes portfolios are used in both curricular and programmatic ways, as in a writing-across-the-curriculum project: for example, to help students see the kinds of evidence, arrangements, and conventions accepted by different discourse communities and to help writers function in one or more of them. Various models for portfolio projects thus do exist (as this collection suggests), and they are helpful, but chiefly to illustrate the possible, not to prescribe or dictate. Any teacher's project or any school's project should be designed to enhance its own curricular aims and agenda, to suit its own writers.

The context will dictate how to determine content and its arrangement so that assessment, pedagogy, and portfolio structure work toward the same ends. Before deciding how to organize the contents, teachers may well want to consider using different kinds of portfolios at different points during the project. What teachers frequently do is to use two kinds of portfolio: (1) a working portfolio and (2) a completed or final portfolio. The working portfolio, as the name suggests, acts as an archive of a writer's work. Characterized more by saturation than by selection, it includes virtually all evidence of a student's work in writing. The completed portfolio, sometimes called a presentational or an exemplary portfolio, can also be created throughout a project, but is finally assembled at the project's conclusion. The final portfolio is ordinarily composed in part of pieces culled from the working portfolio; these pieces constitute a text that can be glossed by the students in one or more metacognitive ways. The writers thus compose a narrative of their own development, in turn creating another view and record of development of their thinking and composing.

The contents and structure of the *working* portfolio are suggested by the aims of the curriculum. For instance, if the overall aim of the course or project is to help the students learn how to write in the private world and the public world, it would make sense to include all finished pieces representing those efforts, as well as incomplete pieces such as previous drafts, invention drafts, and peer response sheets that contributed to those efforts. The working portfolio might well include other pieces, too—excerpts from writing logs, from reader-writer journals, from other classes, again some fragmentary perhaps, but all testament to the writers' development, part of their continuing conversation about writing. It is even possible that the writers will want to include nonscholastic writing in the working portfolio, as David Kneeshaw suggests in Chapter 8, or will be sufficiently motivated to include self-initiated writing. (In fact, including this work might even be one aim of a portfolio project.) In other words, the contents of the working portfolio can be determined on the basis of four types of goals:

1. Specific class or curricular goals
2. Additional goals set by the classroom teacher
3. Multidisciplinary curricular goals
4. Goals set by the student

Because the working portfolio tends to be informal, its contents can be arranged in various ways: by goals; by type of writing (for example, personal or public, narrative or transactional, imaginative); by chronological sequence; by the writer's sense of satisfaction with a piece or a piece's state of completion; or by some other category chosen by the teacher or the writer. Each arrangement, of course, tells us something else about the writer, so more than one arrangement, particularly if attempted inductively, might be tried (Bleich 1988; Graves 1990). Including some sort of summary sheet can help the students set their own course of learning and invite teacher assistance in doing so. On these summary sheets, the students can note their perceptions of certain pieces and their relative status; for instance, "ready for presentational portfolio" or "flawed brilliance, [never] to be tackled again."

The contents and structure of the *completed* portfolio, however, are typically more formal, more clearly defined, and more focused. The completed portfolio is no longer an archive, but a presentation, a performance. Contents and structure are oriented to curricular and audience aims; sometimes these aims and contents are identified early, when the class commences, and sometimes teachers allow writers to determine at least some of the aims and contents as the course progresses. For instance, a teacher may require that students complete three short essays, but each student then selects the one essay to be included in the final portfolio, perhaps after consulting with teacher and peers. In another case, students may be required to include one of several papers written for other classes. In still another case, students may be required to include in the final portfolio one piece for each of the following aims: expressive, transactional, and poetic.

Before making any of these choices, however, the students would have been told, first, the specified number and types of writings to be assembled in the final portfolio, with options as appropriate; and, second, the other kinds of entries that would help the teacher-reader. These could include a "Table of Contents" that outlines the nature and arrangement of the pieces; a "Letter of Acknowledgment" in which the writers thank those who provided assistance and which suggests to the teacher what kinds of assistance the writer found most beneficial (Maimon 1989); a "Grade Justification" entry that argues in favor of a certain grade based on the submitted pieces, presented in the context of this student's performance in this particular class; a metacognitive component representing the "Writer's Reflections" on writing throughout the project; and a culminating "Writer's Profile" that describes and summarizes the writers' composing processes and identifies their perceptions of their strengths and weaknesses as writers, as well as ways to compensate for or adapt to them. Other portfolio components no doubt are possible, but this brief list provides a foundation for thinking about how a completed portfolio might look.

Formative and Summative Readings

Readings of the portfolio entries, like readings of all student work, will vary according to purpose: to help develop, formative; or to evaluate, summative. However, peers, the teacher, and perhaps others read both formal and informal pieces that are in process, long before the completed portfolio is submitted, so that students have the opportunity to rework them. As important, because students may rework their pieces, teachers read these pieces differently than they would in traditional classes. The third principle governing portfolio practice speaks to these methods of reading students' work. What it first suggests is that the institutional response to the pieces—grading, sorting, awarding credit—be deferred as long as possible.

As an institutional mechanism, grading is necessary, of course, and it is not likely that institutions will soon abandon their demands for this form of assessment. Besides, some students are so well socialized that inviting them to defer grades, even temporarily, may increase rather than diminish their anxiety. So teachers in portfolio-based writing classes do not always make the same choices when deciding when to institute grading (as opposed to responding to) their students' work. Some teachers assign grades to pieces throughout the course of a project, allowing students to rewrite only some pieces, or allowing composers to rewrite all of them—for a higher grade. Other teachers do not grade the in-process pieces formally, relying instead on a system of pluses, checks, and minuses to suggest quality, or using a completion grade to award credit for work submitted regardless of quality. Still other teachers prefer to grade only after the final portfolio is introduced. For these teachers, the working portfolio provides texts for learning, the final portfolio texts for both learning and grading.

When teachers are ready to read writing for a grade, however, they need to understand that this purpose in reading affects their students, too, and thus the nature (and the pedagogical value) of the reader-writer transaction is altered. Simply put, in a "graded context," the students will write for one purpose above all, not so much to learn or to try something new, but principally to earn a grade (Britton et al. 1975; Sommers 1982). Likewise, teachers will read not so much to see how their students are developing or to suggest new directions, but to assess, to assign value (Purves 1984). In this situation, teachers' reading of and response to text are directed in large part, first, toward providing such an evaluation and, second, toward providing a justification of the reading and of the assigned grade. When *reading to grade,* then, teachers shift their posture from one of "inquiry reading," in which the goal is to understand and respond as a reader, to one in which the goal is to explain and justify a formal, fixed, and critical assessment. These two reading processes are different processes, and portfolios can distinguish between them and between their functions.

When teachers in portfolio-based writing classes do begin to respond to students' work, they find that their readings are purposeful in new ways. Their initial reason for reading is not to grade an assignment, but to inquire about and to re-create the rhetorical situation, to become the reader invoked by the text, and to generate questions and responses that will help the writer and move the dialogue forward. Inquiry reading is thus rhetorically driven. It does not ask how well a task is completed, but what and how the text means. It seeks to re-create the text and to communicate that re-creation to the writer so that the dialogue initiated by the writer might be continued (Phelps 1989; Watson 1991). Overall, then, inquiry reading is not situated within a presumed ideal text, but rather within writer intent and meaning, its principal operations being questioning and dialogue.

A final issue of portfolio assessment pertains to the summative evaluation that teacher-readers give to the completed portfolios. Teacher practice on this issue is also mixed. Some teachers working within the confines of their own classroom respond to the portfolios by themselves, as they would ordinarily (Yancey et al. 1990). They may assess the portfolio impressionistically and globally, seeing their task as reading not the individual pieces, but the whole. Other classroom teachers read final portfolios more analytically, assessing each individual piece and averaging their scores to determine a portfolio grade. Still other teachers work as members of a group that "blind" rates portfolios as in a holistic scoring session, with two ratings per folder provided (and a third to settle disputes). Sometimes these ratings in effect assign the grade, but in other programs the readings are used to provide a gross discrimination, between proficiency and nonproficiency, for example. In this latter case, once proficiency has been established, the classroom teacher may assign a standard letter grade (Belanoff and Elbow 1986). Other assessments are possible, too, but these indicate the range: from individual teachers adapting current practice to groups of teachers rating together.

Other Benefits

A fourth principle guiding portfolio work suggests that we can actively look for specific benefits to derive from portfolio projects. As described by Belanoff and Elbow (1986) and Burnham (1986), one of the most obvious is that such projects often provide a new vehicle for staff development, particularly when portfolio rating is conducted in groups. During the rating sessions, staff members have the opportunity to discuss issues central to writing, to assessment, to portfolio programs, and to composition studies. What do we value in our students' writing, for instance? How can we foster its development? How do we define the nature of beneficent response? Exploring and discussing such questions benefits teachers and students alike. Even when teachers individually grade their own students' work, however, they can certainly share their insights with other faculty members, and indeed such discussions are often planned.

A second benefit of portfolio practice derives from the framing created by the portfolios; because a student's work is presented within its own context, teachers often see writers' performances and the teacher's task in new and insightful ways. After looking over sets of portfolios, for example, Mary Ann Smith observed that students' work seemed better when they responded to assignments that included a specific audience (1989); perhaps students do try to write to and for those audiences. This seems more likely because in the same students' non-audience-specified pieces the texts read as compositions written for a teacher audience, and they were less successful. In other words, the multiplicity of pieces and assignment types provided for in the portfolios enabled such an observation. Observations like these will help teachers continue to understand how they can best help students. Portfolios may also help teachers better understand the relationship of metacognitive work to formally assigned work. Having students gloss and narrate their own texts and their own histories as writers will enable teachers to see the role that self-awareness plays in the fostering of literacy. This is a new area of exploration, but a promising one.

Portfolio Programs in Process

A final guiding principle of portfolio practice relates to the portfolios themselves: enactments of process and transaction, they are in process as well. Because portfolios are still new and experimental, teachers currently initiate their use with the expectation that the projects should be reviewed and revised and redefined. But even when portfolios are better established as a practice, their practitioners should still routinely consider their aims and uses. Do portfolios as currently conceptualized and defined foster development in writing? Do they help students become (better) writers? What attitudes toward writing do they engender? Are the portfolio contents appropriate, given the aims of the curriculum? Are students given enough authority in selecting the contents of the final portfolio? Are they given enough help in doing so? Are students prepared to assume responsibility for their own writing? Answering questions like these will help teachers assess the usefulness of portfolios relative to their curricular and pragmatic aims. Such an assessment can then be used to modify both portfolios and curricula.

Ultimately, portfolios as a method of teaching, structuring, and responding to writing will themselves need to be assessed. This will become possible as they continue to be used and refined, as their potential becomes understood and better realized. Even now, however, we understand something about them as a type, as a frame, as a practice. Together with portfolios in fields as diverse as art and finance, portfolios in writing classes share common characteristics: they are developmental, diverse in content, and collaborative in composition and ownership. Writing portfolios also are often explicitly metacognitive, inviting writers and readers to perceive new and fruitful relationships among various writings and between these and the author. Because they are oriented to development, they encourage students to take risks and to experiment. And as a pedagogical device, portfolios extend the teacher-student dialogue throughout the course.

Moreover, principles guiding portfolio practice are emerging. Their practitioners tend to be volunteers, and any portfolio project's aims are consistent with curricular and programmatic aims. Such aims help determine appropriate portfolio content and structure. Likewise, portfolios enable a valuable distinction to be made between response to reading and institutional assessment. Such pedagogical response often takes the form of inquiry reading, whose intent is not just to re-create text, but also to continue the dialogue initiated by the writer through the text. Portfolios provide other benefits as well: an opportunity for staff dialogue regarding writing and the opportunity to learn more about writing and ways to teach it. Finally, portfolios themselves are always in revision.

Some Intriguing Questions

The move to portfolios has raised as many questions as it has answered, and these should be mentioned as well. Many of them are being explored now, as they have been from the first. Chief among them are the following:

Precisely what role does reflection play in nurturing the growth of writers? In what other ways might we foster it? Are there points in the development of a writer and in the development of a piece when reflection is most advantageous? When it is not helpful?

What is an appropriate balance between process and product within the portfolio? What kind of processes should be included? Examples of invention? Reflection? Inquiry? Collaboration? How are these related to writing performance?

How can we encourage students to assume more responsibility for their own learning? How can we encourage students to assume responsibility for their peers' learning? How do we help students make wise choices in selecting the contents of their portfolios?

How do students go about deciding which pieces to include in their portfolios? How do they manage competing claims—the need to show improvement, to satisfy themselves, to please the teacher? What happens to their grades when they simply make bad choices? Or choices that do not work for teachers? What happens to these students when they move on to another, more traditional classroom?

How do we go about reading portfolios? What competing insights—regarding processes, student growth, reaction to a given piece, concerns about grade inflation or administrative pressures—inform portfolio readings and assessment? How can we share these readings with our students? Could we develop qualitative responses to be used across a set of portfolios?

What other forms of portfolio assessment might we develop?

As portfolios are reviewed, they should be subject to one last but important question, a question put to assessment generally, as suggested by Peter Johnston at the 1989 NCTE Annual Convention (1989). Johnston suggested then that the salient question to put to any assessment methodology—or to pedagogy, for that matter—is this: Whose needs does it serve to assert this particular view of writing? In terms of portfolio practice, the question might be rephrased this way: Whose needs does it serve to assert the view of writing and writers put forward by the portfolio practitioners represented in this volume? Whose needs are served by viewing writers in process and over time and as capable of helping us help them? Increasingly, the answer seems to be: this view serves us all.

References

Belanoff, P., and P. Elbow. 1986. "Using Portfolios to Increase Collaboration and Community in a Writing Program." *WPA: Writing Program Administration* 9:27–40.

Bleich, D. 1988. *The Double Perspective: Language, Literacy, and Social Relations.* New York: Oxford University Press. See Chapter 6 especially.

Britton, J. N., T. Burgess, N. Martin, A. McLeod, and H. Rosen. 1975. *The Development of Writing Abilities (11–18).* London: Macmillan.

Burnham, C. 1986. "Portfolio Evaluation: Room to Breathe and Grow." In *Training the New Teacher of Composition,* edited by C. Bridges, 125–39. Urbana, Ill.: NCTE.

Crowley, S. 1989. *A Teacher's Introduction to Deconstruction.* Urbana, Ill.: NCTE. See especially Chapter 3.

Graves, D. 1990. "Portfolios, Politics, and Implications." Paper presented at the Annual Convention of the National Council of Teachers of English, Atlanta.

Johnston, P. 1989. "Theoretical Consistencies in Reading, Writing, Literature, and Teaching." Paper presented at the Annual Convention of the National Council of Teachers of English, Baltimore.

Lucas, C. K. 1988. "Toward Ecological Evaluation." *The Quarterly* 10(1):1–17.

Maimon, E. 1989. "Writing and Liberal Education: You Can't Have One without the Other." Curriculum 2000 Series, Purdue University, Lafayette, Ind.

Phelps, L. W. 1989. "Images of Student Writing: The Deep Structure of Teacher Response." In *Writing and Responding,* edited by C. Anson, 37–67. Urbana, Ill.: NCTE.

Purves, A. C. 1984. "The Teacher as Reader: An Anatomy." *College English* 46(3):259–65.

Smith, M. A. 1989. "Portfolio Assessment: Its Promise and Pitfalls." Paper presented at the Annual Convention of the National Council of Teachers of English, Baltimore.

Sommers, N. 1982. "Responding to Student Writing." *College Composition and Communication* 33(2):148–56.

Watson, S. 1991. "Letters on Writing—A Medium of Exchange with Students of Writing." In *Teaching Advanced Composition: Why and How,* edited by K. Adams and J. Adams, 133–51. Portsmouth, N.H.: Boynton/Cook.

Yancey, K., J. Seybold, J. Cox, B. Fusik, and C. Galbraith. 1990. "Variations on a Theme: Portfolios in Three Contexts." Paper presented at the annual fall conference of Indiana Teachers of Writing, Indianapolis, September.

Appendix:
Annotated Bibliography

Sheila C. Ewing
Indiana Department of Education

Books

Belanoff, Pat, and Marcia Dickson, ed. 1991. *Portfolios: Process and Product.* Portsmouth, N.H.: Heinemann, Boynton/Cook.

> Presents a broad introduction to portfolio theory and practice, geared to the college and high school level. Contains sections of articles on "Portfolios for Proficiency Testing," "Program Assessment," "Political Issues," and "Classroom Portfolios."

Bingham, Anne. 1987. "Using Writing Folders to Document Student Progress." In *Understanding Writing: Ways of Observing, Learning, and Teaching,* edited by Thomas Newkirk and Nancie Atwell, 129–35. Portsmouth, N.H.: Heinemann.

> Discusses an elementary teacher's use of writing folders to document both student progress and the success of the writing program. Discusses the value of portfolios to parents, students, teachers, and others.

Educational Testing Service. 1989. *The Student Writer: An Endangered Species?* Focus 23. Princeton, N.J.: ETS.

> Contains a section on "Writing Portfolios," relating ETS's developmental work on using portfolios for writing assessment.

Tierney, Robert J., Mark A. Carter, and Laura E. Desai. 1991. *Portfolio Assessment in the Reading-Writing Classroom.* Norwood, Mass.: Christopher-Gordon Publishers.

> Places portfolios into the context of classroom assessment and presents options for implementing portfolios in the reading-writing classroom. Contains sample materials used in actual classrooms, as well as student examples. Concludes with a broad overview of portfolio use in various situations, from individual classroom to district and state programs.

Articles

Arter, Judy. 1990. "Using Portfolios in Instruction and Assessment: State of the Art Summary." Unpublished paper. Northwest Regional Educational Laboratory, Portland, Oregon. November.

Summarizes state-of-the-art portfolio use for instruction and assessment. Discusses definition, content, self-reflection and self-evaluation, and issues in using portfolios.

Au, Kathryn H., Judith A. Scheu, Alice J. Kawakami, and Patricia A. Herman. 1990. "Assessment and Accountability in a Whole Literacy Curriculum." *The Reading Teacher* 43(April):574–78.

Focuses on the use of reading-writing portfolios as the assessment system for one elementary school's whole literacy curriculum. Describes student portfolios, which are designed to include information on six aspects of literacy and are evaluated in reference to grade-level benchmarks.

Barrs, Myra. 1990. *"The Primary Language Record:* Reflection of Issues in Evaluation." *Language Arts* 67(3):244–53.

Lists some of the newer observation-based methods of assessment, many of which are included in *The Primary Language Record.* Includes writing folders as an example of cumulative records of children's progress.

Bishop, Wendy. 1989. "Qualitative Evaluation and the Conversational Writing Classroom." *Journal of Teaching Writing* 8(2, special issue):267–85.

Suggests that writing teachers add qualitative measures to their repertoire of assessment methods. Describes four manageable writing classroom evaluation measures, one of which is writing portfolios.

Camp, Roberta. 1990. "Thinking Together about Portfolios." *The Quarterly* 12(2):8–14, 27.

Examines changes in teaching and learning that support the use of portfolios as a means of writing assessment. Describes the evolution of the use of portfolios as part of the Pittsburgh Public Schools Arts PROPEL project and shares the thinking of middle school and secondary teachers involved in the project.

Elbow, Peter, and Pat Belanoff. 1986. "Portfolios as a Substitute for Proficiency Examinations." *College Composition and Communication* 37:336–39.

Describes the development and process used by the State University of New York at Stony Brook to implement portfolios in a required writing course as a replacement for proficiency examinations.

Farr, Roger. 1990. "Setting Directions for Language Arts Portfolios." *Educational Leadership* 48(3):103.

Recommends careful consideration before replacing standardized tests with portfolios. Identifies strengths of portfolios when used as informal assessment.

Flood, James, and Diane Lapp. 1989. "Reporting Reading Progress: A Comparison Portfolio for Parents." *The Reading Teacher* 42(March):508–14.

Explains how portfolios might be used to show parents their children's progress in reading. Suggests that reading portfolios should contain test scores, as well as informal assessments, writing samples, self-assessments, and samples of the types of materials students can read at the beginning and end of the school year.

Hiebert, Elfrieda H., and Robert C. Calfee. 1989. "Advancing Academic Literacy Through Teachers' Assessments." *Educational Leadership* 46(7):50–54.

Argues for the use of teacher assessment information, gathered from student portfolios and other records of student progress, to document student achievements in literacy.

Howard, Kathryn. 1990. "Making the Writing Portfolio Real." *The Quarterly* 12(2):1–7, 27.

Describes five phases that middle school students progressed through as they created portfolios: modeling and oral reflection, first written reflection, beginning portfolio, updating portfolio, and finalizing portfolio.

Jongsma, Kathleen Stumpf. 1989. "Questions and Answers: Portfolio Assessment." *The Reading Teacher* 43(December):264–65.

Presents three different brief perspectives on the use of portfolios as a means of evaluating reading and writing.

Kemp, Donald, Winfield Cooper, and Jon Davies. 1991. "The Role of Administration in Portfolio Development." *California Curriculum News Report* 16(3):3–4.

Provides guidelines for administrators as they consider implementing and supporting portfolios in their schools or districts.

Krest, Margie. 1990. "Adapting the Portfolio to Meet Student Needs." *English Journal* 79(2):29–34.

Discusses uses of portfolios for collecting writing, documenting growth, and assessing progress. Offers practical suggestions for adapting portfolio use and grading to students of differing grade, ability, and motivational levels.

Lucas, Katherine Keech. 1988. "Toward Ecological Evaluation, Part Two: Recontextualizing Literacy Assessment." *The Quarterly* 10(2):4–10.

Proposes an ecological model of evaluation that incorporates assessment in the teaching-learning process. Lists portfolio evaluation as one of the practices that supports this model.

Mathews, Jackie. 1990. "From Computer Management to Portfolio Assessment." *The Reading Teacher* 43(February):420–21.

Outlines steps taken by a Florida school district to change to a portfolio literacy assessment.

Meyer, Carol, Steven Schuman, and Nancy Angello. 1990. "Aggregating Portfolio Data." White Paper. Northwest Regional Educational Laboratory, Portland, Oreg. September.

Summarizes key issues and concerns related to aggregating assessment information from portfolios. Presents questions and answers related to each issue.

Mills, Richard P. 1989. "Portfolios Capture Rich Array of Student Performance." *The School Administrator* (December):8–11.

Outlines the steps taken by Vermont to implement a statewide portfolio assessment of writing.

Mumme, Judy. 1989. "Portfolios: An Assessment Alternative." California Mathematics Project, Department of Mathematics, University of California, Santa Barbara, October.

Introduces the idea of using portfolios as an alternative means of assessment in mathematics. Presents possible purposes for mathematics portfolios and suggests their contents. Appendices contain criteria for evaluation and samples of student work.

Murphy, Sandra, and Mary Ann Smith. 1990. "Talking About Portfolios." *The Quarterly* 12(2):1–3, 24–27.

Presents portfolios as a way for teachers to make decisions about what to teach in writing courses and how they want to teach it. Raises questions that must be answered before beginning a portfolio project and offers examples of different ways that three schools answered the questions.

Paulson, F. Leon, Pearl R. Paulson, and Carol A. Meyer. 1991. "What Makes a Portfolio a Portfolio?" *Educational Leadership* 48(5):60–63.

Defines *portfolio* and offers eight guidelines for achieving the potential of portfolios, namely, self-directed student learning.

"Performances and Exhibitions: The Demonstration of Mastery." 1991. *Horace* 6(3):1–12.

Discusses portfolios as a means of recording achievement produced through performances and exhibitions. Includes the example of Walden III's Rite of Passage portfolio of required pieces.

"Portfolios Illuminate the Path for Dynamic, Interactive Readers" (Secondary Perspectives). 1990. *Journal of Reading* 33(May):644–47.

Discusses benefits of keeping portfolios to document students' strengths and growth in reading. Includes sample charts and forms.

Rief, Linda. 1990. "Finding the Value in Evaluation: Self-Assessment in a Middle School Classroom." *Educational Leadership* 47(6):24–29.

Considers portfolios as a way for teachers to learn what students are able to do and how they are able to do it and, more importantly, as a way for students to become self-evaluators.

Simmons, Jay. 1990. "Adapting Portfolios for Large-Scale Use." *Educational Leadership* 47(6):28.

Reports results of research indicating that self-selected portfolios of students' best work are significantly better than timed tests in estimating writing ability.

Simmons, Jay. 1990. "Portfolios as Large-Scale Assessment." *Language Arts* 67(March):262–67.

Describes a research project comparing single, timed writing samples to portfolios of students' work. Concludes that portfolios can be used for large-scale assessment of writing and provide a fairer and more accurate profile of student writers.

Solomon, Gwen. 1991. "Electronic Portfolios." *Electronic Learning* 10(5):10.

Describes an experimental program for storing portfolios on computer disks so that "electronic portfolios" may follow students to high school graduation in order to assess growth over time.

Stenmark, Jean Kerr. 1989. "Assessment Alternatives in Mathematics: An Overview of Assessment Techniques That Promote Learning." Berkeley: University of California (EQUALS and California Mathematics Council *Campaign for Mathematics*).

Includes portfolios as a means of assessing authentic achievement in mathematics. Describes contents and benefits of student portfolios in mathematics.

Valencia, Sheila. 1990. "A Portfolio Approach to Classroom Reading Assessment: The Whys, Whats, and Hows." *The Reading Teacher* 44(January):338–40.

Argues for a portfolio approach to reading assessment and describes how a reading portfolio might look, how it might be organized, and how it might be used.

Vavrus, Linda. 1990. "Put Portfolios to the Test." *Instructor* 100(1):48–53.

Leads classroom teachers through five decision areas for implementing portfolio-based assessment in the classroom: what it will look like, what it will contain, how and when to select, evaluating portfolios, and passing them on.

"Vermont Writing Assessment: The Pilot Year." 1990. Vermont Department of Education, Montpelier, September.

> Outlines the Vermont plan for using portfolios to assess writing at Grades 4 and 8. Includes description of portfolio contents, criteria for evaluation, and information about reporting results.

Wiggins, Grant. 1989. "Teaching to the (Authentic) Test." *Educational Leadership* 46(7):41–47.

> Mentions portfolios as one type of exhibition of mastery, or authentic test. Includes an example of a portfolio that is part of a final exhibition required for a diploma from a member of the Coalition of Essential Schools.

Wolf, Dennie Palmer. 1989. "Portfolio Assessment: Sampling Student Work." *Educational Leadership* 46(7):35–39.

> Provides background and rationale for the development of the portfolio assessment system used in the Arts PROPEL project. Identifies the distinguishing characteristics of Arts PROPEL portfolios and discusses the benefits of using portfolios.

Newsletters

Portfolio Assessment Newsletter. Five Centerpointe Drive, Suite 100, Lake Oswego, Oregon 97035.

> Published five times a year by the Northwest Evaluation Association to support an information network for educators interested in portfolios and portfolio assessment.

Portfolio News. c/o San Dieguito Union High School District, 710 Encinitas Boulevard, Encinitas, California 92024.

> Published by the Portfolio Assessment Clearinghouse, each issue contains reports of individual projects and discussions of issues of concern in portfolio assessment.

Portfolio—The Newsletter of Arts PROPEL. Harvard Project Zero, 323 Longfellow Hall, Harvard Graduate School of Education, 13 Appian Way, Cambridge, Massachusetts 02138.

> Published by Arts PROPEL, a project dedicated to fostering artistic development in middle and secondary school students, this newsletter promotes dialogue between researchers from ETS and Harvard Project Zero and teachers of music, visual arts, and imaginative writing.

Editor

Kathleen Blake Yancey is assistant professor of English at the University of North Carolina at Charlotte. A former middle school language arts teacher, she currently teaches undergraduate courses in freshman and advanced composition, reading and literature, and methods of teaching English, as well as graduate courses in the teaching of English and in writing assessment. She is affiliated with the National Writing Project and is a continuing consultant for the Indiana Assessment Committee. She is a frequent presenter at conferences (NCTE, CCCC, ITW), has published in various journals, and regularly consults with public school and university faculty to help them design curricula and assessment.

Contributors

Roberta Camp, a development scientist at the Educational Testing Service (ETS) for twelve years, studies traditional and experimental approaches to writing assessment. Before joining ETS, she taught composition and literature at the community college level in Pennsylvania. Recently, her work has focused on portfolio approaches to assessment and on classroom activities that promote student self-assessment. She now codirects the development of writing curriculum and assessment in the Arts PROPEL project for the Pittsburgh Public School District. She is also a principal member of the ETS team that is developing software-delivered modules for critical thinking in the language arts.

Catherine D'Aoust is codirector of the Writing Project at the University of California, Irvine, and coordinator of Instructional Services in Saddleback Valley Unified School District. She taught high school English for nine years and currently coordinates language arts instruction (K–12). She teaches a seminar on the teacher-as-researcher, in which she and her students collaborate on classroom-based research. She is a frequent presenter at conferences and Writing Project sites and has contributed two book chapters on writing as a process.

Sheila C. Ewing is K–12 language arts consultant with the Indiana Department of Education in Indianapolis, where she works with statewide curriculum and assessment programs. She currently coordinates a network of portfolio model sites and is redesigning the state writing assessment program. A former secondary English teacher and college writing instructor, she is completing her doctorate at Purdue University.

Sue Ellen Gold teaches English and social science at Irvine High School in Southern California. She is a teacher consultant for the Office of Teacher Education at the University of California, Irvine (UCI), and a member of the UCI Writing Project research team, where she has been developing multicultural curricula. She has contributed to texts such as *Practical Ideas for Teaching Writing as a Process* (published by the California State Department of Education) and *Thinking/Writing: Fostering Critical Thinking through Writing* (in press). She is currently part of a state-funded research team working on restructuring high school education.

David Kneeshaw is assistant coordinator of communications, ESL, ESD for the East York Board of Education, Toronto, Ontario. He taught high school and junior high school English and was an English department head at two East York schools. He has coauthored six junior-level, whole-language readers and authored nine novel study guides. Since 1985 he has led a series of courses in the writing process for teachers.

He has spoken at IRA, CCTE, and local board conferences from Newfoundland to Alberta. Under his leadership, various school boards publish annual anthologies of students' writing and art, as well as periodic anthologies of teachers' writing.

Catharine Lucas is professor of English and composition coordinator at San Francisco State University. She has taught high school English, trained secondary teachers of English, and served as writing assessment consultant to educational groups in the United States and Canada. A former staff member and current fellow of the Bay Area Writing Project, she collaborated with teacher-researchers to produce three monographs evaluating teaching practices and with Leo Ruth and Sandra Murphy on the study described in their *Designing Writing Tasks for the Assessment of Writing*. Her writing on assessment issues has appeared in *The Quarterly* of the National Writing Project and the Center for the Study of Writing and in reports from the National Testing Network in Writing. She has been a regular presenter at NTNW, AERA, CCCC, and CCTE.

Sandra Murphy is associate professor and director of the Center for Cooperative Research and Extension Services for Schools in the Division of Education at the University of California, Davis. She teaches graduate-level courses on the teaching of reading and writing and has taught high school English and freshman composition. She coauthored *Designing Writing Tasks for the Assessment of Writing* (with Leo Ruth) and *Writing Portfolios* (with Mary Ann Smith) and has written several articles on the acquisition of reading and writing. She is also a consultant to educational organizations on the assessment of writing.

James E. Newkirk is an assistant principal at Western Heights Middle School in Hagerstown, Maryland. He taught middle school language arts at Clear Spring Middle School for fifteen years and was Washington County's middle school writing resource teacher for two years. As a teacher consultant for the Maryland Writing Project, he makes presentations throughout the state and within his own county school system.

Mary Ann Smith is director of the California Writing Project and vice president and treasurer of the National Writing Project Nonprofit Corporation. Before these appointments, she was the director of the Bay Area Writing Project. For several years, she taught English, Grades 7 through 12, and was a staff development specialist in the Mt. Diablo Unified School District in Concord, California. Author of several articles on the teaching and assessment of writing and on the contributions of National Writing Project teachers, she is coauthor, with Sandra Murphy, of *Writing Portfolios*.

Irwin Weiser is associate professor of English and director of composition at Purdue University, where he teaches a practicum in teaching composition, graduate courses in the rhetoric and composition program, and undergraduate writing courses. He is the author of a freshman rhetoric, *Writing: An Introduction,* and coauthor of *Language and Writing: Applications of Linguistics to Rhetoric and Composition.* He has published in the *Journal of Teaching Writing, WPA,* the *Arizona English Bulletin,* and *Freshman English News* and has served on the editorial boards of *WPA, Journal of Teaching Writing,* and *Journal of Basic Writing.*